# Structure & Speaking Practice
# Istanbul

**NATIONAL
GEOGRAPHIC**

L E A R N I N G

Australia • Brazil • Mexico • Singapore • United Kingdom • United States

National Geographic Learning,
a Cengage Company

**Structure & Speaking Practice, Istanbul**

**Becky Tarver Chase**

Publisher: Sherrise Roehr

Executive Editor: Laura LeDréan

Managing Editor: Jennifer Monaghan

Digital Implementation Manager,
Irene Boixareu

Senior Media Researcher: Leila Hishmeh

Director of Global Marketing: Ian Martin

Regional Sales and National Account
Manager: Andrew O'Shea

Content Project Manager: Ruth Moore

Senior Designer: Lisa Trager

Manufacturing Planner: Mary Beth
Hennebury

Composition: Lumina Datamatics

Student Edition: Structure & Speaking Practice, Istanbul
ISBN-13: 978-0-357-13797-0

**National Geographic Learning**
20 Channel Center Street
Boston, MA 02210
USA

Locate your local office at **international.cengage.com/region**

Visit National Geographic Learning online at **ELTNGL.com**
Visit our corporate website at **www.cengage.com**

Printed in China
Print Number: 02   Print Year: 2019

# Photo credits

# Scope and Sequence

| | Unit Title & Theme | Listenings & Video | **ACADEMIC SKILLS**<br>Listening & Note Taking |
|---|---|---|---|
| **1** | **TECHNOLOGY TODAY AND TOMORROW**<br>*page 1*<br><br>ACADEMIC TRACK:<br>Technology | **Lesson A**<br>A Radio Show about AI<br><br>**VIDEO**<br>Can Robots Learn to Be More Human?<br><br>**Lesson B**<br>A Conversation about Technology | • Identifying Important Details<br>• Using Abbreviations |
| **2** | **A THIRSTY WORLD**<br>*page 21*<br><br>ACADEMIC TRACK:<br>Environmental Science | **Lesson A**<br>A Talk about the Itaipu Dam (with slide show)<br><br>**VIDEO**<br>Dam-Release Rafting<br><br>**Lesson B**<br>A Discussion about the Ogallala Aquifer | • Listening for Problems and Solutions<br>• Using a T-Chart |
| **3** | **SPECIES SURVIVAL**<br>*page 41*<br><br>ACADEMIC TRACK:<br>Life Science | **Lesson A**<br>A Talk about Birds (with slide show)<br><br>**VIDEO**<br>Amazing Chameleons<br><br>**Lesson B**<br>A Conversation about a Photo Project | • Listening for Repeated Words<br>• Re-Writing Your Notes |

| Speaking & Presentation | Vocabulary | Grammar & Pronunciation | Critical Thinking |
|---|---|---|---|
| • Giving Reasons<br>• Making Eye Contact<br>**Lesson Task**<br>Discussing Self-Driving Cars<br>**Final Task**<br>Presenting a New Technology Product | Using Collocations | • Action and Nonaction Verbs<br>• Stressed Content Words | **Focus**<br>Synthesizing<br><br>Analyzing, Brainstorming, Evaluating, Interpreting a Bar Graph, Organizing Ideas, Personalizing, Prior Knowledge, Reflecting |
| • Asking for and Giving Opinions<br>• Speaking at the Right Volume<br>**Lesson Task**<br>Presenting a Clean Water Device<br>**Final Task**<br>Role-Playing a Meeting | Recognizing Suffixes | • Active and Passive Voice<br>• Suffixes and Syllable Stress | **Focus**<br>Prioritizing<br><br>Analyzing, Applying, Evaluating, Interpreting a Map, Organizing Ideas, Personalizing, Predicting, Prior Knowledge |
| • Talking about Causes and Effects<br>• Timing Your Presentation<br>**Lesson Task**<br>Presenting a Life Lesson<br>**Final Task**<br>Presenting a Research Proposal | Identifying the Correct Definition | • Phrasal Verbs<br>• Stress in Multi-Syllable Words | **Focus**<br>Personalizing<br><br>Analyzing, Organizing Ideas, Prior Knowledge |

Independent Student Handbook, p. 61      Vocabulary Index, p. 76

# TECHNOLOGY TODAY AND TOMORROW

# 1

People play the game Pokémon
Go on their mobile phones in
La Villette Park in Paris, France.

## ACADEMIC SKILLS

| | |
|---|---|
| LISTENING | Identifying Important Details |
| | Using Abbreviations |
| SPEAKING | Giving Reasons |
| | Stressed Content Words |
| CRITICAL THINKING | Synthesizing |

## THINK AND DISCUSS

1 What are the people in the photo doing? Have you ever
tried this game or other games for mobile phones?

2 What's the title of this unit? What are some things you
think you will learn about in this unit?

## EXPLORE THE THEME

**Look at the photos and read the information. Then discuss these questions.**

1. Have you ever heard or read about any of the topics on these pages? Explain.
2. In 1968, how did movie audiences feel about AI? How do you feel about it? Why?
3. Do you know of any ways that you use AI in your daily life? Explain.
4. How do you think AI might impact our future?

# MOMENTS IN AI HISTORY

Artificial Intelligence, or AI, is a machine's ability to "think" and perform tasks that are typically done by human beings. Although AI may seem like a very modern concept, it has been around for much longer than many people realize.

▶ **2011:** IBM's Watson computer beats its human competitors at the popular TV quiz show *Jeopardy!*

**2016:** The Mercedes Benz F 015 self-driving car stands at Dam Square in Amsterdam, the Netherlands.

**1968:** Movie audiences decide that AI is dangerous when HAL, the computer in *2001: A Space Odyssey*, decides that keeping itself "alive" is more important than the lives of the astronauts.

**1950:** British mathematician, computer scientist, and codebreaker Alan Turing (far left) proposes the Turing test to determine a computer's ability to "think."

# A Vocabulary

MEANING FROM CONTEXT **A** 🎧 **Track 1** Read and listen to the information. Notice each word in **blue** and think about its meaning.

## Timeline of AI History

**1950**

**1960**

**1970**

**1980**

**1990**

**2000**

**2010**

**2020**

**1950:** In *I, Robot*, a book of fictional[1] short stories by Isaac Asimov, the makers of robots **command** them not to harm humans. The robots, however, sometimes create their own rules depending on the **circumstances**.

**1950s:** Computers become a **practical** tool for doing calculations quickly, and since they don't make any mistakes, they are more **reliable** than humans.

**1956:** Researchers at Dartmouth College say they **intend** to study "**artificial** intelligence" during a two-month summer conference.

**1997:** A computer called Deep Blue wins a chess match against world champion Garry Kasparov, and it's clear that computers can go **beyond** just following instructions and can actually "think" for themselves. In the past, programmers had to **instruct** computers in great detail and tell them exactly what to do.

**2011:** A computer called Watson **replaces** one of the humans competing on the TV quiz show *Jeopardy!*—and wins! Watson is **capable** of understanding spoken questions.

**2016:** Google puts together a group of engineers in Switzerland to research "machine learning," an important part of artificial intelligence.

[1] **fictional** (adj): not real; from the author's imagination

**B** Complete each question with a word from the box. Use each word only once.

| capable (adj) | instruct (v) | intend (v) | reliable (adj) | replace (v) |
|---|---|---|---|---|

1. Do you think computers are usually _____, or do they often not work?

2. What are some of the things most computers are _____ of doing?

3. In what kinds of jobs do you think robots might _____ human beings?

4. What does your English teacher often _____ the class to do?

5. What do you _____ to do after class?

**C** Work with a partner. Take turns asking and answering the questions from exercise B.

**D** Match each word with its definition.

1. _____ command (v)　　　　　a. to tell someone or something what they must do
2. _____ circumstances (n)　　b. useful or sensible
3. _____ practical (adj)　　　　c. farther than
4. _____ artificial (adj)　　　　d. conditions which affect what happens in a
　　　　　　　　　　　　　　　　　 situation
5. _____ beyond (prep)　　　　e. created by human beings, not by nature

---

**VOCABULARY SKILL** Using Collocations

*Collocations* are words that are frequently used together. Knowing which words to collocate, or combine, will help you use new words correctly and make your English sound more fluent.

| | |
|---|---|
| *be capable of* | *Intelligent machines* **are capable of** *making decisions.* |
| *intend to* | *Do you* **intend to** *register for the history course?* |
| *under (the, any, etc.) circumstances* | *I'm afraid of robots. I wouldn't get one* **under** *any* **circumstances**! |

---

**E** Underline the collocations in the questions below. Then discuss the questions in a group.

CRITICAL THINKING: ANALYZING

A: *I'm not sure whether computers are capable of thinking.*
B: *The timeline information makes me think they're not that smart yet.*

1. Do you think computers are (or will be) capable of thinking in the same way that human beings do? Explain.

2. Can you imagine life now without computers or the Internet? How would life be different under those circumstances?

3. What homework or assignments do you need to do? When do you intend to do them?

# A Listening A Radio Show about AI

## BEFORE LISTENING

PRIOR KNOWLEDGE **A** Work with a partner. Discuss these questions.

1. Which Internet search engines do you use? Why?
2. Do you do much shopping online? If so, what kinds of things do you buy?
3. How do doctors or hospitals use computers?

## WHILE LISTENING

LISTENING FOR MAIN IDEAS **B** 🎧 **Track 2**  Listen to the radio show and choose the answer that best completes each statement.

1. Artificial intelligence plays a role when you are _____.

   a. sending an email message          b. searching the Internet

2. Machine learning could enable computers to _____.

   a. follow our instructions          b. discover something new

3. Intelligent computers could help doctors by _____.

   a. reading a lot of information          b. communicating with patients

▼ **Tourists communicate with guidance robot "Kaiba" at Haneda Airport in Tokyo, Japan. The airport aims to put these robots into use in 2019.**

When listening to a talk or interview, it's important to identify which details you need to include in your notes. The most important details are the ones that will help you understand and remember the speaker's main ideas. Here are some questions you can ask yourself to help you identify the most important details: *Does this information clarify or explain a main idea? Does the speaker emphasize this information? Does the speaker repeat this information?*

When you take notes, you often need to write down information very quickly. You can do this by writing down only key words and phrases. Another technique you can use is to take notes using abbreviations. Here are some common abbreviations you can use:

year → *yr*   with → *w/*   because → *b/c*   for example → *e.g.*   in other words → *i.e.*

before → *b/f*   technology → *tech.*   medical → *med.*   artificial intelligence → *AI*

You can also abbreviate words and phrases by writing down only consonants.

people → *ppl*     computer → *cmptr*     students → *stdnts*

There are many ways to use abbreviations when taking notes. The most important thing is to develop a system that works for you.

**C** 🎧 **Track 2** Listen again. Take notes on the one or two details you think are the most important for each main idea. Use abbreviations.

NOTE TAKING

1. Main idea: Artificial intelligence limits Internet search engine results.

   _____

2. Main idea: Search engines are capable of a kind of thinking.

   _____

3. Main idea: Intelligent computers could help in the medical field, for example with cancer.

   _____

## AFTER LISTENING

**D** Work with a partner. Compare and discuss your notes from exercise C. How did you decide which detail or details were the most important? Which words did you abbreviate and how?

**E** Discuss these questions with your partner.

CRITICAL THINKING: REFLECTING

1. Have you experienced the kind of intelligent search engine the radio-show guest describes?
2. How do you feel about computers that can possibly think and make decisions?

# A Speaking

## GRAMMAR FOR SPEAKING  Action and Nonaction Verbs

### Action Verbs

*Action verbs* show physical or mental activities.

| bring | compare | eat | increase | replace | respond | work |
|-------|---------|-----|----------|---------|---------|------|
| build | decide | happen | occur | run | speak | worry |

### Nonaction Verbs

*Nonaction verbs* describe states and conditions. Most nonaction verbs tell us about states of mind, emotions, the senses, or possession. We usually do not use nonaction verbs with the present continuous.

Here are some common nonaction verbs:

| be | hear | love | need | remember | think |
|----|------|------|------|----------|-------|
| believe | know | matter | own | see | understand |
| have | like | mean | prefer | seem | want |

| Action Verbs | Nonaction Verbs |
|--------------|-----------------|
| We **are learning** about computer science. | We **know** how to program computers. |
| Rita **is watching** people in the coffee shop. | She **sees** one person she knows. |
| I **am listening** to one of my favorite songs. | I **hear** a violin. |

Some verbs can be both action verbs and nonaction verbs, but the meanings are different. Use the grammar and context clues to understand the meaning.

> I **am thinking** about my sister. She **thinks** homework is a waste of time.
> We **have** a lot of food in the house. We**'re having** a dinner party tonight.

**A** Read each sentence and look at the underlined verb form. Is it correct? Write C for *correct* and I for *incorrect* on the line after each sentence. Then make any necessary corrections.

1. My professor <u>thinks</u> that AI will benefit the medical field. _____

2. Many people <u>are believing</u> that AI is dangerous. _____

3. They <u>are working</u> on a new app this month. It will help children learn math. _____

4. These days, more scientists <u>are researching</u> cancer and diabetes. _____

5. How many pairs of shoes <u>are you owning</u>? _____

6. If the food is good, it <u>isn't mattering</u> if the restaurant is far away. _____

7. I can't talk right now. We <u>have</u> dinner. _____

8. Are you OK? You <u>seem</u> upset. _____

**A woman takes a photo with her smartphone at sunrise.**

**B** Work with a partner. Discuss these questions. Use the correct verb forms. PERSONALIZING

1. What kind(s) of "smart" devices are you using these days? How are you using them?
2. Do you think it's a good idea for young children to use smartphones and computers?
3. What are some things you understand and don't understand about computers and AI?
4. What do you want from a smartphone? From a computer?
5. What are you reading in the news about computers and robots these days?
6. How do you feel about AI? Does it make you worried or optimistic? Explain.

**SPEAKING SKILL** Giving Reasons

It's important to give reasons when you want to support your opinions or explain a set of circumstances. Here are some words and phrases you can use to give reasons. Notice how *because* and *since* can connect clauses and show the relationship between ideas.

> Cancer is a problem for doctors **because** it's really many diseases—not just one.
> **Since** computers can read a lot of information very quickly, they might be able to discover new things.

Here are some other phrases that introduce reasons:

> **For this reason**, I'm worried about programs that track my behavior online.
> **Another reason** for my concern is the lack of privacy online.

**C** Complete each sentence so it is true for you. Then read and discuss your sentences with a partner. PERSONALIZING

1. Because I am studying English, _____ .

2. _____ since all of my friends are using cell phones.

3. I enjoy spending time with my best friend because _____ .

4. Since I'm a(n) _____ person, I usually _____ .

5. My family lives in _____ . For this reason, _____ .

# LESSON TASK  Discussing Self-Driving Cars

PERSONALIZING **A** Work in a group. Read the information about self-driving cars. Then discuss the questions below.

> **SELF-DRIVING CARS**
>
> Many new cars are already offering automation. Examples include automatic parallel parking, automatic braking in emergencies, and lane-assist warnings to tell drivers if their car crosses a solid line on the road. Now, companies are testing completely automatic cars that don't require a driver. These cars are expected to become popular in some parts of the world in the near future.

1. Have you ever read about self-driving cars, or have you seen one? Is the idea of self-driving cars interesting to you? Explain.
2. What forms of transportation do you usually use? What are some of the advantages and disadvantages of the forms of transportation you use?

CRITICAL THINKING: EVALUATING **B** With your group, discuss the pros and cons of self-driving cars. Then add some of your own ideas to the T-chart.

| Pros | Cons |
|---|---|
| • **Safety**: Most traffic accidents are caused by people driving dangerously. | • **High cost**: The new technology will be far too expensive for most people. |
| • **Fewer traffic jams**: Unlike some people, self-driving cars could communicate and cooperate with each other. | • **Less privacy**: Computers will need to keep a lot of data on people's activities. |
| • **More transportation options**: People who are unable to drive could use self-driving cars. | • **The unexpected**: Computers in self-driving cars can't be programmed for every possibility, for example understanding hand signals from a police officer. |
| Your ideas: | Your ideas: |
| • _____ | • _____ |
| • _____ | • _____ |
| • _____ | • _____ |
| • _____ | • _____ |
| • _____ | • _____ |
| • _____ | • _____ |

This Volkswagen "Sedric" self-driving automobile was displayed at the 87th Geneva International Motor Show in Geneva, Switzerland in March 2017.

**C** Work in a group. Look at the bar graph and discuss the questions below. Give reasons to support your ideas.

CRITICAL THINKING: INTERPRETING A BAR GRAPH

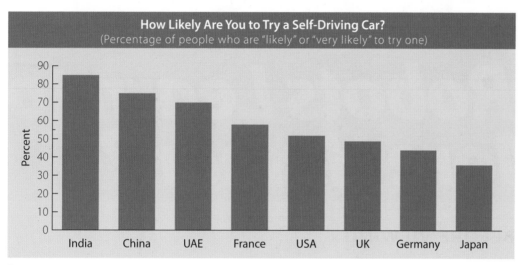

**How Likely Are You to Try a Self-Driving Car?**
(Percentage of people who are "likely" or "very likely" to try one)

Source: www.statista.com

1. What information does this bar graph show?
2. Which country has the highest percentage of people who are likely or very likely to try a self-driving car? Which country has the lowest percentage?
3. Is your country represented on the bar graph? If so, does the information surprise you? Why or why not?
4. Think of possible reasons for people being likely or unlikely to try self-driving cars.

**D** As a group, discuss these questions. Give reasons to support your ideas.

CRITICAL THINKING: REFLECTING

1. How likely are you to try riding in a self-driving car? Explain.
2. After discussing question 1, has anyone in the group changed their mind about self-driving cars?

**E** Work with the whole class. Tell your teacher how many people in your group are likely to try riding in a self-driving car. Then discuss these questions.

CRITICAL THINKING: ANALYZING

1. What percentage of people in your class are likely to try a self-driving car? How does that percentage compare with the percentages in the bar graph in exercise C?
2. What does this information tell you about the people in your class?

# Video

A robot soccer referee gives a player a red penalty card. The robot soccer players are able to sense their surroundings and respond to other players' movements.

# Can Robots Learn to Be More Human?

## BEFORE VIEWING

CRITICAL THINKING:
ANALYZING

**A** Work with a partner. Look at the photo and read the caption. Then discuss these questions.

1. Describe what you see. What is happening in the photo?
2. Do you think that robots can learn to be more human? Explain.

**B** Match each word or phrase with its meaning. You may use a dictionary. You will hear these words and phrases in the video.

1. _____ human features (n)
2. _____ compelling (adj)
3. _____ barriers to entry (n)
4. _____ accessibility (n)
5. _____ natural language commands (n)
6. _____ remote presence device (n)

a. how easy something is for people to use
b. spoken words that tell machines what to do
c. a machine that can be somewhere that a person can't be
d. body parts that people have, such as eyes, ears, and arms
e. things that prevent people from using something
f. convincing

**C** Read the information about Chad Jenkins. With a partner, discuss ways that robots could help human beings. If you had a robot, what would you ask it to do for you?

CRITICAL THINKING: ANALYZING

> **MEET CHAD JENKINS.** He's a National Geographic Explorer, a computer scientist, and roboticist. His research group at Brown University in the U.S. is looking for ways that robots can help human beings and improve their lives. One aspect of Jenkins's research involves teaching robots though demonstration. This means that instead of using computer codes to program robots, people simply show the robot a behavior, and the robot learns it. Jenkins appreciates the progress that's been made in computer science, but he thinks the progress in robotics will be even more impressive in the future. When it comes to robotics, he says, "We have more wisdom about the technology to do it better."

## WHILE VIEWING

**D** ▶ **1.1** Read the statements. Then watch the video and choose T for *True* or F for *False*. Correct the false statements.

UNDERSTANDING DETAILS

1. The human features that Jenkins mentions are eyes and ears.   T   F
2. Jenkins says that robots might be able to help elderly (very old) people.   T   F
3. One of the barriers to entry that Jenkins mentions is cost.   T   F
4. In order to control a robot, you need to be a computer programmer.   T   F
5. The video shows the remote presence device inside Jenkins's home.   T   F

**E** ▶ **1.1** Read the quotes from the video. Then watch the video again and fill in the blanks with the information you hear.

UNDERSTANDING DETAILS

1. "Traditionally I've worked in the area of robot _____ from demonstration…"
2. "There's many different ways you can actually _____ a robot."
3. "A much _____ approach is to just take the robot's arm and guide the robot's arm…"
4. "Another approach is to treat the robot as a remote-control _____."
5. "We'd love to make it based on what we call natural language _____…"
6. "Robotics is really an extension of the _____ Technology Revolution…"

## AFTER VIEWING

**F** Discuss these questions in a group.

CRITICAL THINKING: ANALYZING

1. What are three ways robots could help elderly or disabled people (e.g., people who are not able to see or walk)?
2. What are three ways robots could help other people in their daily lives?
3. If you had a robot, how do you think it could improve your life?

# B Vocabulary

MEANING FROM CONTEXT **A** 🎧 **Track 3** Read and listen to the information. Notice each word or phrase in **blue** and think about its meaning.

## SAVING THE ENVIRONMENT IN GERMANY

Germany has a history of caring about the environment, but it's a country with a lot of industry that **consumes** enormous amounts of coal. When coal and other **fossil fuels** such as petroleum are burned, they send **carbon** into the air, and carbon is the main cause of climate change. In order to fight air pollution and climate change, Germans have **cut back on** the amount of coal they use. As part of this effort, they are also using cleaner energy sources such as solar and wind power.

**Innovative** forms of technology, including enormous wind turbines and huge numbers of solar panels, are helping Germany reach its goal of having only 20 percent of its energy come from fossil fuels by the year 2050. The change has been **gradual**—beginning in the 1970s—and it hasn't been easy. Many environmental groups as well as **individual** people in Germany have spent a lot of time and money on clean energy.

## CHANGING LIVES IN INDIA

Around 1.1 billion people **worldwide** live without electricity, and about 25 percent of those people live in India. Solar energy—in the form of small lights that get their power from the sun—is now solving problems for many of them. This innovative technology lets small businesses stay open at night, so people in India are earning more money. In addition to the positive economic **impact**, the air inside homes is cleaner since people are not burning wood or kerosene[1] for light. Solar power is also a good **alternative** to expensive batteries[2] that need to be replaced. With the help of innovative technology, people in rural villages can live more like people in large cities.

[1]**kerosene** (n): a liquid fuel made from petroleum
[2]**batteries** (n): small devices that provide electrical power

A couple in India holds a solar powered lamp during their wedding ceremony.

**B** Write each word or phrase in **blue** from exercise A next to its definition.

1. _____ (n) something that can be used instead of another thing
2. _____ (n) coal, petroleum, and natural gas
3. _____ (adv) existing or happening throughout the world
4. _____ (adj) relating to just one person or thing
5. _____ (adj) new and original
6. _____ (n) a chemical element that coal and diamonds are made of
7. _____ (phrasal v) to reduce
8. _____ (n) effect
9. _____ (adj) happening slowly over time
10. _____ (v) uses something up

**C** Work with a partner. Take the quiz. Then check your answers below.

CRITICAL THINKING: ANALYZING

### QUIZ: WHAT'S YOUR SOLAR-POWER I.Q.?

1. Which system consumes the most energy in most homes?

   a. electronics   b. heating and cooling rooms   c. water heating   d. refrigeration

2. Which energy source sends the most carbon into the air?

   a. oil (petroleum)   b. coal   c. natural gas   d. solar power

3. Which alternative to fossil fuels produces the most power in the United States?

   a. wind   b. solar   c. geothermal[1]   d. wood

4. How much does the addition of solar equipment increase the value of a home in the United States?

   a. $1,000   b. $2,000   c. $7,000   d. $17,000

5. When was the innovative technology that makes solar panels work invented?

   a. 1940s   b. 1950s   c. 1970s   d. 1980s

Source: worldwildlife.org

[1]**geothermal** (adj): related to heat found deep inside the earth

**D** Work in a group. Discuss these questions.

CRITICAL THINKING: EVALUATING

1. What are some ways people can cut back on the amount of energy they use?
2. Who do you think has a more significant impact when it comes to using less energy or using alternative forms of energy: individual people or groups (e.g., companies or governments)? Explain.
3. Germany wants 80 percent of its power to come from innovative technology such as solar, wind, and biofuels by the year 2050. Do you think that goal is realistic for your country? Explain.

**Answers:** 1. b, 2. b, 3. a, 4. d, 5. d

# Listening A Conversation about Technology

## BEFORE LISTENING

**A** 🎧 **Track 4** Read and listen to information about an innovative solution to a problem in Baltimore, USA.

---

### BALTIMORE'S MR. TRASH WHEEL

With innovative technology, we can solve old problems in new ways. One old problem was the trash from the city of Baltimore, Maryland, that ended up in the Jones Falls River. The river flows into Baltimore's Inner Harbor—a popular tourist destination—and from there into the Chesapeake Bay and the Atlantic Ocean.

Meet Mr. Trash Wheel, a device that uses the motion of river water and energy from solar panels to collect plastic bottles, cigarette butts, carry-out food containers, and other garbage from the river. Baltimore's Inner Harbor is now a more attractive place for visitors. Hundreds of tons of trash have been removed from the water system, and other communities are thinking about building their own trash wheels.

---

CRITICAL THINKING:
INTERPRETING
A GRAPHIC

**B** Look at the graphic below. Then match each part of Mr. Trash Wheel with its function.

1. _____ floating booms
2. _____ rotating forks
3. _____ waterwheel
4. _____ solar panels
5. _____ Dumpsters

a. turn the wheel when the water is moving slowly
b. direct floating trash toward the forks
c. collect and hold the trash from the conveyor belt
d. pick up trash from the water, put it on the conveyor belt
e. uses movement of river water to move the conveyor belt

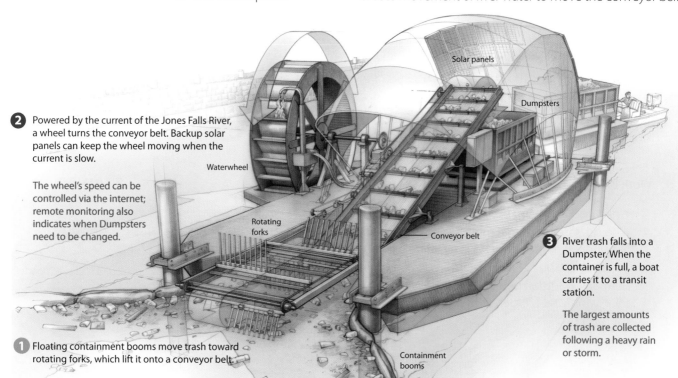

**2** Powered by the current of the Jones Falls River, a wheel turns the conveyor belt. Backup solar panels can keep the wheel moving when the current is slow.

The wheel's speed can be controlled via the internet; remote monitoring also indicates when Dumpsters need to be changed.

Waterwheel

Rotating forks

Solar panels

Dumpsters

Conveyor belt

**3** River trash falls into a Dumpster. When the container is full, a boat carries it to a transit station.

The largest amounts of trash are collected following a heavy rain or storm.

**1** Floating containment booms move trash toward rotating forks, which lift it onto a conveyor belt.

Containment booms

# WHILE LISTENING

LISTENING FOR MAIN IDEAS

**C** 🔊 **Track 5** Listen to the conversation. Then answer the questions.

1. What two kinds of energy does the trash wheel use? _____

2. Which part of Mr. Trash Wheel is a very old kind of technology?

   _____

3. What kind of new technology is making people like Mr. Trash Wheel?

   _____

LISTENING FOR DETAILS

**D** 🔊 **Track 5** Listen again. Choose the correct word or phrase to complete each sentence.

1. The (city / boat) takes away the Dumpsters when they are full of trash.
2. Mr. Trash Wheel catches (50 / 90) percent of the trash from the river.
3. One kind of trash that is mentioned is (soda / garbage) cans.
4. People online suggested adding (eyes / ears) to the trash wheel.
5. Several other communities (are building / might build) trash wheels.

# AFTER LISTENING

> **CRITICAL THINKING** Synthesizing
>
> When you synthesize, you combine, or put together, information from two or more sources in order to understand a topic in a new way. This can also involve combining new information with your own ideas and knowledge about a topic. Synthesizing can help you find a solution to a problem or think of new ways of doing or improving something.

CRITICAL THINKING: SYNTHESIZING

**E** Work with a partner. Discuss this question: What are three ways the Internet is used to operate or promote Mr. Trash Wheel? Use information from the conversation and the graphic on page 16. Write your ideas in the chart.

| Mr. Trash Wheel's Success: Three Ways the Internet Is Used | | |
|---|---|---|
| 1. | 2. | 3. |

CRITICAL THINKING: SYNTHESIZING

**F** Form a group with another pair of students. Compare your answers from exercise E. Then discuss this question: How could the Internet and other new kinds of technology be used to help Mr. Trash Wheel have an even bigger impact on the environment?

# B Speaking

CRITICAL THINKING:
ANALYZING

**A** With your partner, look at the types of technology listed in the box, and ask and answer the questions below.

A: *What's changing with TV or movies?*

B: *People are watching them on their phones, but they're still going to the movie theater, too.*

| apps/programs | cameras | computers | the Internet | phones | TV/movies | other |
|---|---|---|---|---|---|---|

1. What is happening or changing with each kind of technology these days?
2. How do people use each kind of technology to solve problems in their daily lives?
3. In your country, what impact are cell phones or other devices having on your culture? For example, are these devices changing education, or the ways people make money or make new friends?

---

**EVERYDAY LANGUAGE**  Giving Advice

*You **should** create a stronger password for your wi-fi.*

*You **shouldn't** work so hard.*

*We **had better** get back to work.*

*Luisa **had better not** forget to set her alarm. She has an early exam.*

---

CRITICAL THINKING:
EVALUATING

**B** Read each statement and choose A for *Agree* or D for *Disagree*.

1. People shouldn't check their phones when they're doing things with their friends or family.   A   D

2. Governments should make sure everyone in their country has access to the Internet.   A   D

3. People had better not share their personal information online.   A   D

4. Engineers should invent some inexpensive devices so that everyone can afford them.   A   D

5. App designers should focus on helping to solve people's problems, rather than entertaining them with games.   A   D

▶ **Men using their cell phones, Bali Island, Indonesia**

**C** Work in a group. Take turns saying the statements in exercise B aloud and whether you agree or disagree. Give reasons for your opinions.

PERSONALIZING

---

**PRONUNCIATION** Stressed Content Words

🎧 **Track 6** In English, not every word in a sentence gets the same amount of stress or emphasis. Content words receive more stress because they have more meaning or give more information than other words. This means the stressed syllable in content words is a bit louder, longer, and higher in pitch. Content words include:

nouns      main verbs      adjectives

adverbs      question words

*The **book** is on the **table** in the **back** of the **room**.*
*My **friend took** a **chemistry course** in **college**.*

---

**D** Underline the content words in each sentence.

1. Nabila is taking a course in computer programming.
2. Samir wants to become a software designer.
3. All of my friends have cell phones.
4. Large televisions consume a lot of electricity.
5. I'm trying to cut back on the time I spend online.
6. Kenji wants to buy a phone with a better camera.

**E** 🎧 **Track 7** Listen to the sentences from exercise D and check your answers. Then practice saying the sentences with a partner. Remember to stress the content words.

## FINAL TASK  Presenting a New Technology Product

You are going to give a short pair presentation. You and a partner will think of a real problem and a new kind of technology product that could help solve that problem. Your job is to convince your audience that the idea is good and the product is worth buying.

**A** Work with a partner. Brainstorm a list of problems that you care about. The problems could be major issues that your community or the world is dealing with (e.g., pollution, crime, or traffic), or they could be smaller everyday problems (e.g., oversleeping, forgetting vocabulary words, or being late). Write the list in your notebook.

BRAINSTORMING

**B** Look at your list of problems and choose one that you both want to focus on.

**C** Brainstorm ideas for new technology products that could help solve the problem you chose in exercise B.

BRAINSTORMING

**D** Choose one of your ideas from exercise C and create a proposal for a new kind of technology product. It should be for a product that doesn't exist yet. Think about what the product will do, its name, who will want to buy it (e.g., children, doctors, governments), and any other important details. Complete the proposal outline below with brief notes as you plan your presentation.

---

**Proposal Outline**

a. Description of problem: _____

b. Product description (name of product; How does it solve the problem?):

    _____

c. Target market (Who will buy it? Who is it for?): _____

d. Other details (price, location, etc.): _____

e. Conclusion (Summarize the product's benefits.): _____

---

**E** Decide who will present which information. Write brief notes to use during your presentation. Use the information from your proposal to help you. Then practice your presentation. Give reasons to support your ideas, and remember to stress content words.

---

**PRESENTATION SKILL** Making Eye Contact

When you are giving a presentation, it's important to look up from your notes often and speak directly to your audience. If it's a small group, try to make brief eye contact with each person. If it's a large group, be sure to look toward every part of the room at least once. This will make people want to listen to you and will help you connect with your audience.

---

**F** Give your presentation to the class. Remember to make eye contact with your audience.

---

# REFLECTION

1. What are some useful vocabulary collocations you learned in this unit?

    _____

    _____

2. What do you think is the most innovative kind of technology discussed in this unit?

    _____

    _____

3. Here are the vocabulary words and phrases from the unit. Check (✓) the ones you can use.

| | | |
|---|---|---|
| ☐ alternative AWL | ☐ consume AWL | ☐ instruct AWL |
| ☐ artificial | ☐ cut back on | ☐ intend |
| ☐ beyond | ☐ fossil fuel | ☐ practical |
| ☐ capable AWL | ☐ gradual | ☐ reliable AWL |
| ☐ carbon | ☐ impact AWL | ☐ replace |
| ☐ circumstance AWL | ☐ individual AWL | ☐ worldwide |
| ☐ command | ☐ innovative AWL | |

# A THIRSTY WORLD

Three million black plastic balls help turn away the sun's UV rays and protect the drinking water in the Ivanhoe Reservoir in Los Angeles California, USA.

ACADEMIC SKILLS

LISTENING  Listening for Problems and Solutions
Using a T-Chart
SPEAKING  Asking for and Giving Opinions
Suffixes and Syllable Stress
CRITICAL THINKING  Prioritizing

THINK AND DISCUSS

1  Look at the photo. What do you think these people are doing?

2  Which do you think is a bigger problem—too much water, or not enough water?

21

**Look at the infographic and read the information. Then discuss the questions.**

1. What is *Hidden Water*, or *virtual water*?

2. How many gallons of water are required to produce a cup of tea? A pair of jeans? A T-shirt? A pound of figs?

3. Which kind of diet requires more water: a mostly vegetarian diet or a diet that includes meat? Why?

4. Does any of the information from the infographic surprise you? Will it cause you to change any of your everyday habits?

# HIDDEN WATER

The world consumes trillions of virtual gallons of water. When you serve a pound of beef, you are also serving 1,857 gallons[1] of water. A cup of coffee? That's 37 gallons, enough water to fill the average bathtub. When you wear a pair of jeans, you're wearing 2,900 gallons.

This is the amount of fresh water that we consume but don't actually see. It's called *virtual water:* the amount of water used to create a product.

[1]one gallon = 3.785 liters

**ANIMAL PRODUCTS**
Virtual-water totals include the amount of water used to raise the animals and make the product into food (e.g., making milk into cheese).

**589**
PROCESSED CHEESE

**400**
EGGS

**371**
FRESH CHEESE

**138**
YOGURT

**MEAT**
The virtual water for meat is the water the animals drink and the water used to grow their food and clean their living areas.

**1,857**
GALLONS OF WATER USED TO PRODUCE ONE POUND OF BEEF

**469**
CHICKEN

## FRUITS AND VEGETABLES

Both rainwater and irrigation water are included in the virtual-water totals for fruits and vegetables.

## EVERYDAY ITEMS

Cotton is used to make many items that we wear and use every day, such as T-shirts, jeans, and bedsheets, and it requires a lot of water.

**2,900**
GALLONS TO
PRODUCE ONE PAIR
OF BLUE JEANS

**379**
GALLONS FOR A
POUND OF FIGS

**154** AVOCADOS

**109** CORN

**193**
PLUMS

**43** BEANS

POTATOES
**31**

**25** EGGPLANTS

**185**
CHERRIES

**103** BANANAS

APPLES
**84**

GRAPES
**78**

ORANGES
**55**

**33** STRAWBERRIES

**2,800**
ONE COTTON
BEDSHEET

**766**
ONE COTTON
T-SHIRT

**634**
ONE BURGER

**53**
ONE GLASS
OF MILK

**9**
ONE
CUP
OF TEA

**37**
ONE
CUP OF
COFFEE

## WHY MEAT USES MORE WATER

A human diet that regularly includes meat requires 60 percent more water than a mostly vegetarian diet. This is due to the amount of water needed to raise cattle. The graphic on the right shows the amount of water needed to raise an average cow (approximately 3 years).

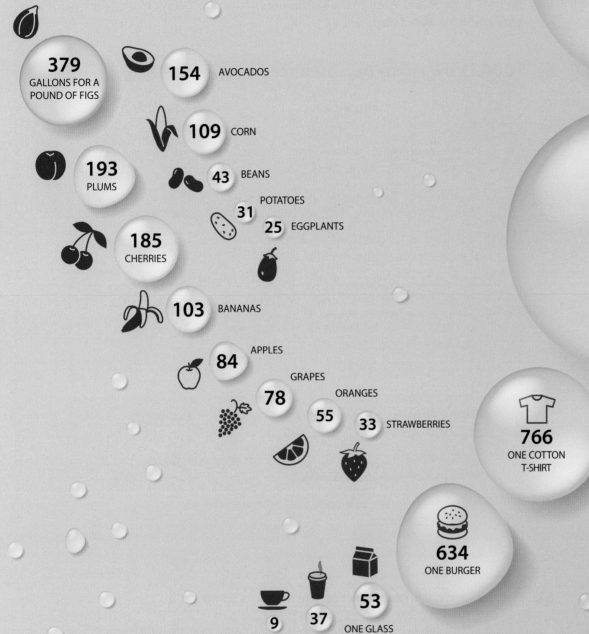

**88,400**
GALLONS FOR
18,700 POUNDS
OF FEED

+

**6,300**
GALLONS
FOR
DRINKING

+

**1,900**
GALLONS FOR
CLEANING

=

**816,600**
GALLONS USED
DURING THE LIFE OF
THE ANIMAL

# A Vocabulary

**A** 🎧 **Track 8** Read and listen to the statements in the quiz below. Notice each word in **blue** and think about its meaning.

---

## QUIZ: HOW MUCH DO YOU KNOW ABOUT WATER?

1. The Amazon River **supplies** about 20% of the fresh water that enters the world's oceans.    T    F

2. Farmers **require** 911 gallons (3,450 liters) of water to produce 2.2 pounds (1 kilogram) of rice.    T    F

3. The **risk** of disease is high if the water you drink is not clean. About 1 million people die each year from drinking dirty water.    T    F

4. Farming uses a **significant** amount of water—up to 40 percent of the fresh water used worldwide.    T    F

5. The United States has built more than 80,000 dams[1] to **manage** water for different uses such as producing electricity.    T    F

6. Scientists say that 13 gallons (50 liters) of water per day is **adequate** for one person.    T    F

7. You can **collect** water in a desert with just a sheet of plastic and an empty can.    T    F

8. Water is a renewable **resource**, so we can use the same water again and again.    T    F

9. The Nile River in Africa (the longest river in the world) **flows** through four different countries.    T    F

10. People in Australia use the smallest **amount** of water of any country in the world.    T    F

---

[1]**dam** (n): a wall built across a river to stop the water from flowing, often to make electricity

**B** Match each word in **blue** from exercise A with its definition.

| | | |
|---|---|---|
| 1. _____ supplies (v) | a. | material people can use |
| 2. _____ require (v) | b. | how much there is of something |
| 3. _____ risk (n) | c. | possibility that something bad will happen |
| 4. _____ significant (adj) | d. | enough |
| 5. _____ manage (v) | e. | moves slowly without stopping |
| 6. _____ adequate (adj) | f. | to bring together |
| 7. _____ collect (v) | g. | gives or provides something |
| 8. _____ resource (n) | h. | to need |
| 9. _____ flows | i. | important, meaningful |
| 10. _____ amount (n) | j. | to use carefully |

A hiker filters water in the Talkeetna Mountains near Palmer, Alaska, USA.

**C** Take the quiz from exercise A. Choose T for *True* or F for *False* for each statement.

**D** Work with a partner. Compare and discuss your answers from the quiz. Then check your answers at the bottom of this page.

---

**VOCABULARY SKILL** Recognizing Suffixes

Adding a suffix to a word changes its part of speech, or grammatical function. For example, the suffixes *-ion /-tion/-ation*, *-ance/-ence,* and *-ment* change verbs to nouns. Recognizing suffixes and parts of speech can help you build your vocabulary.

| Verb | Noun |
|------|------|
| preserve | preservation |
| govern | government |
| occur | occurrence |

---

**E** Choose the correct form of the word to complete each sentence. Then compare your answers with a partner's.

1. Chemistry 101 is a (require / requirement) for my major, so I have to take the course.
2. I have an interesting (collect / collection) of stamps from different countries.
3. Where I live, rainstorms (occur / occurrence) frequently in summer.
4. We (depend / dependence) on fresh water for many things in our daily lives.
5. Good water (manage / management) can help our city during the dry season.
6. Desert plants (require / requirement) very little water to grow.

**F** Work in a group. Discuss these questions.

CRITICAL THINKING: ANALYZING

1. What are the risks of not having enough water? Of having too much water? Do you know of any places that have experienced these problems recently?
2. Besides water, what are some things you require each day?
3. How is the water supply in your country? Is it difficult to get an adequate amount of clean water where you live?
4. Good management of natural resources can make them last longer. Besides water, what are some natural resources that people need to manage well?

**Answers:** The false statements are 3. (about 6 to 8 million people die each year), 4. (around 70 percent of fresh water is used for farming), 9. (11 different countries), and 10. (Mozambique, in Africa).

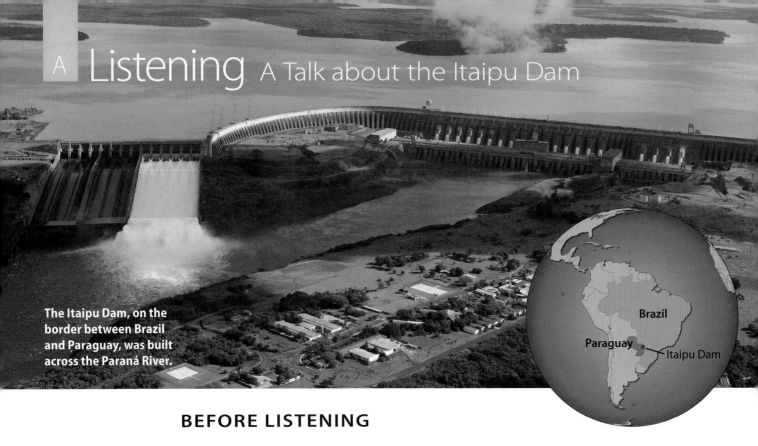

# A Listening A Talk about the Itaipu Dam

The Itaipu Dam, on the border between Brazil and Paraguay, was built across the Paraná River.

Brazil

Paraguay

Itaipu Dam

## BEFORE LISTENING

PRIOR KNOWLEDGE

**A** Work with a partner. Look at the map and photo, and discuss these questions.

1. What do you know about Brazil and Paraguay? Have you ever been to those countries or read news stories about them?
2. The photo shows the Paraná River behind the Itaipu Dam. Can you explain what a dam such as this does?

## WHILE LISTENING

LISTENING FOR MAIN IDEAS

**B** 🎧 **Track 9** ▶ 2.1 Listen to a talk and check (✓) the main idea.

☐ The Itaipu Dam is one of the largest dams in the world.

☐ Building the Itaipu Dam forced many families to leave their land.

☐ The Itaipu Dam is good for the economies of Brazil and Paraguay.

☐ There are both benefits and problems with the Itaipu Dam.

---

**NOTE-TAKING SKILL** Using a T-Chart

Using a T-chart is a helpful way to take notes on two aspects of a topic such as benefits and problems, advantages and disadvantages, or facts and opinions. Having your notes organized in a T-chart is also helpful when you need to review or study the information later.

| Farming | |
|---|---|
| Benefits | Problems |
| produces food | requires a lot of water |

🎧 **Track 9** Listen to the talk again, and complete the notes in the T-chart with the information you hear.

| Itaipu Dam (Paraná River, Paraguay and Brazil) | |
|---|---|
| Benefits | Problems |
| – Building the dam created jobs: about _____ workers were required. <br>           **1** <br><br> – Good for economy: <br><br>   1. Provides about _____ % <br>                    **2** <br>     of the electricity used in Brazil and <br>     about _____ % in Paraguay. <br>             **3** <br><br>   2. Tourist attraction: _____ can <br>                       **4** <br>     go on free tours and go _____ <br>                          **5** <br>     in natural areas. <br><br> – Supplies water that _____ can <br>                         **6** <br>   use during times of drought. | – Reservoir covered _____ square <br>                    **7** <br>   miles of _____ with water. <br>            **8** <br><br> – Around _____ families lost their <br>          **9** <br>   _____ and had to leave the area. <br>      **10** <br><br> – Some _____ and <br>         **11** <br>   _____ sites now underwater. <br>      **12** <br><br> – Farmers say reservoir may be raising <br>   _____ temperatures by as much <br>      **13** <br>   as 4°C. <br><br> – Not everyone thinks the _____ <br>                              **14** <br>   between the two countries is <br><br>   _____ . <br>      **15** |

## AFTER LISTENING

D Work with a partner. Decide which person (or people) would agree with each of the statements below. Then discuss the statements and give reasons for the ones you agree with.

1. _____ The problems with the dam are more significant than the benefits it provides.

2. _____ It might be necessary for some families to lose their land if the result is electricity for many people.

3. _____ The benefits of the dam are more significant than the problems.

4. _____ More countries should build very large dams to manage their water.

a. The guest speaker

b. A family who lost their land

c. The owner of a tourism company near the dam

d. A farmer who grows food crops near the dam

e. You

# A Speaking

---

## GRAMMAR FOR SPEAKING  Active and Passive Voice

In the active voice, the subject performs or does the action.

> The dam **provides** electricity for many people.

In the passive voice, the subject receives the action.

> Electricity **is provided** by the dam.

We form the passive voice with the verb *be* plus the past participle of a verb.

> The water in our city **is managed** carefully.
>
> How **is** this word **pronounced**?

We often use the passive voice to talk about processes.

> Water **is collected** in containers and **used** for washing clothes.

We use *by* with the passive when we want to specify *who* or *what* did the action.

> These books were given to us **by the school**.

---

**A**  Underline the verb form in each sentence. Choose P for *Passive Voice* or A for *Active Voice*. Then complete each sentence to make it true.

1. Rice <u>is grown</u> in countries such as _____          P    A
   and _____ .

2. In my country, a lot of electricity is provided by _____ .          P    A

3. Nowadays, many people study online instead of in _____ .          P    A

4. At my house, we use a significant amount of water          P    A
   for _____ .

5. In my country, children are taught to _____ .          P    A

6. My favorite dish is made with _____ .          P    A

**B**  Work with a partner. Take turns saying and explaining your sentences from exercise A.

> **>** *Rice is grown in countries such as India and Thailand.*

**C**  Take turns asking and answering these questions with a partner. Use the passive voice in your answers.

> **>** *Coffee is grown in Brazil, Colombia, . . .*

1. Where does coffee grow?
2. Who owns or rents the house or apartment next to yours?
3. Who manages the money in your household?
4. What are some of the ways people use smartphones?
5. What kind of people collect coins?
6. Who corrects the homework in this class?

## PRONUNCIATION Suffixes and Syllable Stress

🎧 **Track 10** When the suffixes *-tion*, *-ity*, *-ial*, and *-ical* are added to words, the stress changes. The syllable just before each of these suffixes receives the main stress, or primary stress.

Paying attention to suffixes and syllable stress can help you improve your listening comprehension and pronunciation skills.

| *-tion* | *-ity* |
|---|---|
| **e**ducate → edu**ca**tion | a**vai**lable → availa**bi**lity |
| *-ial* | *-ical* |
| **in**dustry → in**dus**trial | **hi**story → his**tor**ical |

**D** 🎧 **Track 11** Underline the syllable with the main stress in each **bold** word. Then listen and check your answers.

1. **po**litics       It was a significant **po**li̲tical event.
2. **res**ident     This is a **residential** apartment building.
3. **ap**ply       We turned in our **application** before the due date.
4. **pos**sible    There is a **possibility** of finding water on other planets.
5. **in**form      We need more **information** before we make a decision.
6. **the**ory      This is only a **theoretical** situation. It's not real.

**E** Work with a partner. Take turns reading the sentences from exercise D aloud. Pay attention to the suffixes and syllable stress.

**F** Take turns asking and answering these questions with a partner. Pay attention to suffixes and syllable stress.

PERSONALIZING

1. Many people enjoy being active. What are some of the activities you like to do in your free time?
2. People define the word *busy* in different ways. What is your definition of *busy*?
3. Parents influence their children in important ways. Who else has been influential in your life?
4. Many people want to conserve electricity. What are some devices you use that consume a significant amount of electrical power?

# LESSON TASK  Presenting a Clean Water Device

CRITICAL THINKING:
EVALUATING

**A**  Work in a group. Read the situation below and the information about three clean water devices on this and the next page. Use the information to say sentences about each device. Use the passive voice. Then discuss the questions that follow.

> *The drum is used to bring clean water to houses.*

> **Situation:** You work for an organization called Safe Water Now. Your organization wants to spend $1 million for a new device that will help provide clean water for people. You have to give a presentation to the directors of your organization that explains which device is best and why.

1. What problem does each device try to solve?
2. Who could benefit from each device?
3. How easy or difficult do you think it is to make each device and get it to people?

---

**Device 1**  The **Q Drum** carries 13 gallons (50 liters) of water easily.

- drum/use to bring clean water to houses
- rope/put through a hole
- drum/pull/not carry
- drums/make/in South Africa
- drums/sell for $70

---

**Device 2**  The **KickStart Pump** helps farmers provide more water for their crops.

- pump/sell to farmers in Africa
- pump/operate with your feet
- more crops/grow with the water
- money from crops/use for family's health and education
- pumps/make in Kenya/sell for $70

**Device 3** The **LifeStraw** provides clean water for one person for a year.

- LifeStraw/use with any kind of dirty water
- one end/put in a person's mouth/the other end/put into water
- LifeStraw/use in emergency situations and for camping
- no electrical power/require to use the LifeStraw
- LifeStraw/make by a Swiss company/sell for about $20

**A man uses a LifeStraw in Yosemite National Park, California, USA.**

**B** With your group, follow the steps below to plan your presentation.

ORGANIZING IDEAS

1. Decide which device you will present to the directors.
2. Plan what you will say. Use the passive voice when appropriate. Your presentation should answer these questions:

   - Which device did your group choose?
   - How does the device work?
   - Who will this device help? How will it help them?
   - Why do you think this is the best device?

     > *It's easier to use because the drum is pulled, not carried.*

     > *More crops can be grown with the water from the pump, which helps farmers.*

3. Decide which information each member of your group will present.
4. Write notes to help you with your part of the presentation.
5. Practice your presentation.

**PRESENTATION SKILL** Speaking at the Right Volume

When you are giving a presentation, you need to speak a little louder than normal so your audience can hear and understand you. This also shows that you are confident. At the beginning of your presentation, check your volume with your audience. Here are some questions you can ask:

*Can everyone hear me?*      *Is my volume OK?*

**C** With your group, give your presentation to the class. Remember to speak at the right volume.

PRESENTING

## Video

**Dam-Release Rafting**

Whitewater rafters,
Grand Canyon,
Arizona, USA

## BEFORE VIEWING

**A** Read the information about the video you are going to watch. Use your dictionary to help you with any words you don't know.

> **MEET JONNY PHILLIPS AND RICHARD AMBROSE.** They're industrial scientists from the United Kingdom. They are also the hosts of a BBC documentary television show called *I Didn't Know That,* and they're known for doing dangerous and exciting activities. In this video, Jonny and Richard introduce us to an unusual kind of water sport: dam-release[1] rafting. In a country that's not known for its mountainous landscapes, this may be the only way to experience the excitement of whitewater rafting[2].

[1]**release** (v): to let go or set free
[2]**whitewater rafting** (n): rafting that takes place on fast-moving rivers with rough water

PREDICTING    **B** Check (✓) the things you think you will see or learn about in the video. Then compare your predictions with a partner's.

☐ a dam      ☐ a mountain      ☐ how water is released from a dam
☐ a raft      ☐ a river or stream      ☐ how to stay safe when rafting

# WHILE VIEWING

**C** ▶ 2.2 Watch the video and check your predictions from exercise B.

CHECKING PREDICTIONS

**D** ▶ 2.2 Watch the video again and complete each quote from the video with the number that you hear.

UNDERSTANDING DETAILS

1. "This valve alone can release over _____ liters of water a minute."

2. "For water to be released for a whole day, it can cost _____ pounds."

3. "With the dam open, the amount of water flowing down this river increases to a massive _____ million liters."

4. "That's _____ times the normal amount, which means the boys will be traveling down it _____ times faster than normal!"

# AFTER VIEWING

**E** Use the passive form of the verbs in parentheses to complete the steps for dam-release rafting.

1. First, a release of water __is requested__ (request).

2. Second, money _____ (pay) for the release of water.

3. Next, a valve inside the dam _____ (open) to release the water.

4. After that, people in the raft _____ (carry) on a wild ride down the river.

5. Finally, the valve _____, (close) and much of the water stays behind the dam again.

**F** Work with a partner. Close your books and take turns retelling the steps for dam-release rafting from exercise E. Use the passive voice.

**G** Work in a group. Discuss these questions.

CRITICAL THINKING: ANALYZING

1. The kind of rafting you saw in the video is somewhat risky, and people can be hurt if they do it. Why do you think some people enjoy risky or even dangerous activities?

2. Is rafting a sport you might want to do? Explain.

3. Do you think there are any disadvantages to releasing the water from a dam for a water sport? Explain.

# B Vocabulary

PERSONALIZING

**A** Work with a partner. Discuss these questions.

1. Have you ever experienced a water shortage? Explain.
2. Are there any rules in your country about using water? Explain.

MEANING FROM CONTEXT

**B** 🎧 **Track 12** Look at the map and read and listen to the information about "water-stressed areas" in the world. These are areas where the demand for clean water is greater than the supply. Notice each word in **blue** and think about its meaning.

1. An **urgent** problem in the western United States is low levels of groundwater.

2. Water from rivers can be **distributed** to cities and farms where the water is needed.

3. Without adequate water for **agriculture**, a world food **crisis** is possible. If farmers do not have enough water for their crops, it could affect millions of people.

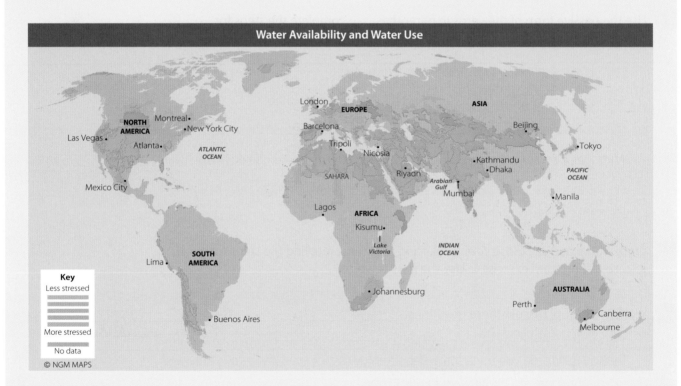

**Water Availability and Water Use**

Key
Less stressed

More stressed

No data
© NGM MAPS

4. Farmers can **reduce** the amount of water they use. Learning about and practicing water **conservation** will allow them to do the same work with less water.

5. Parts of northern Africa are **extremely** dry. For example, the **average** yearly rainfall in the Sahara Desert is less than 1 inch (25 mm).

6. Water is **scarce** in many regions of the world, and people in these areas often do not have access to clean water.

7. Australia has **experienced** both drought and floods in recent years. This has been very difficult for the farmers there.

**C** Complete each definition with the correct word in **blue** from exercise B.

1. If you _____ (v) something, you moved it from one place to many other places.

2. _____ (n) means not using too much of a natural resource.

3. If something is _____ (adj), it is usual and normal.

4. _____ (n) is the science of growing plants and raising animals on farms.

5. If something is _____ (adj), you need to take care of it very soon.

6. A _____ (n) is a large and serious problem.

7. To _____ (v) something means to make it smaller or less.

8. If you _____ (v) something, it happened to you.

9. "_____" (adv) means to a very great degree.

10. If something is _____ (adj), there isn't a lot of it available.

---

**EVERYDAY LANGUAGE**   Showing Interest

In conversation, it is polite to show interest. Here are some phrases you can use:

*Really?*        *That's interesting.*        *Uh-huh.*        *I didn't know that.*        *Wow!*

---

**D** Work in a group. Say whether you agree or disagree with each of the statements below. Be sure to explain and give reasons for your opinions.

PERSONALIZING

1. I need to reduce the amount of water I use.
2. When there's a water crisis, it's usually caused by nature.
3. Not having enough clean water is an urgent problem in my country.
4. Water conservation is extremely important.

**E** Work with a partner. Look at the map and the key on the previous page and complete the exercise.

CRITICAL THINKING: INTERPRETING A MAP

1. According to the map, what are three places where the water situation is urgent (very water stressed)? _____  _____  _____

2. According to the map, what are three places that are not experiencing a water crisis. (less water stressed)?

   _____  _____  _____

3. List two places where the water situation is bad, but not extremely bad.

   _____  _____

4. Describe the water situation in your country according to this map. Do you agree with the information on the map? Explain.

# Listening A Discussion about the Ogallala Aquifer

## BEFORE LISTENING

**A** Read the information in the box. Then answer the questions below with a partner.

> **AQUIFERS**
>
> Aquifers are areas of rock under the ground that contain large amounts of water. Sometimes this water is easy to reach, but often it has to be pumped up out of the aquifer with a special device. In dry parts of the western United States, farmers use water from aquifers to irrigate their fields. Without this water, the fields might be too dry to grow certain food crops.

1. In your own words, what is an *aquifer*?
2. How do farmers in the western United States use the water from aquifers?
3. Why is the water from aquifers so important to these farmers?
4. Do you know of any other places where there are aquifers? If so, where?

## WHILE LISTENING

LISTENING FOR
MAIN IDEAS

**B** 🎧 **Track 13** Listen to the students' discussion and choose the correct answers.

1. What is the topic of the group presentation?

   a. Better Ways to Distribute Water      c. How to Solve the Aquifer Crisis
   b. What Caused the Aquifer Crisis

2. There is an "aquifer crisis" because _____.

   a. the water in the aquifer is difficult to reach      c. the water in the aquifer isn't clean
   b. people are using the aquifer water too quickly

3. Dryland farming is a possible solution to the aquifer crisis because _____.

   a. it requires little water      c. it's a good way to grow corn
   b. it's less expensive for farmers

**Tractors put corn into huge piles at a feedlot near Imperial, Nebraska, USA.**

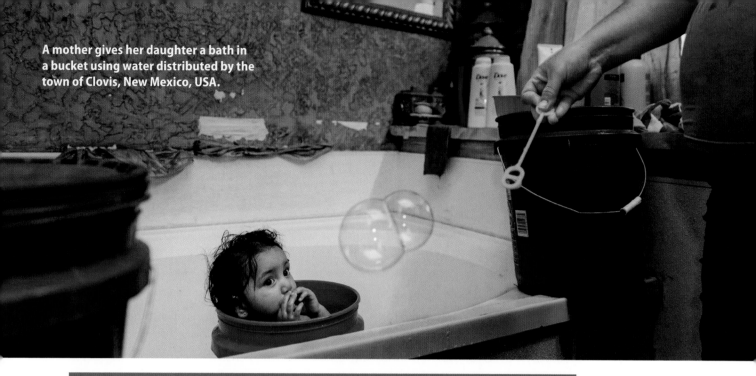

A mother gives her daughter a bath in a bucket using water distributed by the town of Clovis, New Mexico, USA.

---

**LISTENING SKILL** Listening for Problems and Solutions

When listening to a talk or discussion about an issue, being able to recognize and link problems to their solutions will help you understand key ideas about the topic. When listening, pay attention to words and phrases that signal when a speaker is going to talk about a problem or a solution. Here are some examples:

*The problem is* ...          *That's* **one possible solution**, *but* ...

*Here's the issue.*          *Maybe* **the best approach** *is* ...

---

**C** Track 13 Listen to the discussion again and complete the notes in the T-chart.

| The Ogallala Aquifer | |
|---|---|
| Problems | Possible Solutions |
| – Water in aquifers being pumped out quickly (past 70 yrs.) | – Better ways to _____ |
| – In parts of the western U.S., not enough water for <br> 1. _____ <br> 2. _____ | – Water _____ |

## AFTER LISTENING

**D** Work in a group. Compare your notes from exercise C. Then discuss these questions.

1. Which of the two solutions do you think would have more of an impact?
2. What other solutions might there be to the problems the students discussed?
3. What experiences have you had with group projects? Do you think the three students you heard were working together well? Explain.

CRITICAL THINKING: EVALUATING

# B Speaking

> **SPEAKING SKILL** Asking for and Giving Opinions
>
> Here are some expressions you can use to ask people for their opinions:
>
> *Do you think…?*      *What's your opinion of…?*
>
> *What do you think about…?*      *How do you feel about…?*
>
> Here are some expressions you can use when giving your opinion:
>
> *I think…   I feel that…   In my opinion,…   I don't think…   If you ask me,…*

ASKING FOR AND
GIVING OPINIONS

**A** Work with a partner. Take turns asking for and giving opinions about the topics below. Then talk about some of your own ideas.

A: *What do you think is the most interesting sport to watch in the Olympic Games?*
B: *In my opinion, it's skiing. I love watching the skiing events. How about you?*

| | | |
|---|---|---|
| sports in the Olympic Games | traveling to other countries | the weather today |
| owning a car | classical music | online classes |

CRITICAL THINKING:
APPLYING

**B** Work in a group. Read the situation in the box, and look at the information in the chart below. Then discuss the questions on the next page. Use the expressions in the Speaking Skill box to ask for and express opinions.

> **Situation:** Your family lives in a small house. A large water pipe in your city broke yesterday, so there will be less water available to you until the pipe is fixed. It will take the city one whole week to fix the pipe. Each person in your family can use only 13 gallons (50 liters) of water a day, or a total of 91 gallons (350 liters) a week.

## How much water do you need to . . .

 **. . . drink every day?**
.5 gallons/2 liters a day

 **. . . wash the dishes?**
8 gallons/30 liters

 **. . . wash fruits and vegetables?**
2 gallons/8 liters

 **. . . flush the toilet?**
3.5 gallons/13 liters

 **. . . do a load of laundry?**
22 gallons/85 liters

 **. . . take a four-minute shower?**
30 gallons/113 liters

 **. . . brush your teeth?**
.25 gallons/.5 liters

 **. . . wash your face or hands?**
.5 gallons/2 liters

1. What uses of water do you think are absolutely necessary every day?
2. What uses of water do you think are important, but perhaps not necessary every day?
3. What do you think are the best ways for your family to conserve water?

> **CRITICAL THINKING**   Prioritizing
>
> When you have to make difficult decisions, it's important to be able to prioritize and evaluate which of your options is most important. This can help you to determine which things are most important in a certain situation and which things you need to do first.

**C** Make a list of your family's water priorities. Then make a plan for how you will use water for a week. Remember to take notes and do the necessary arithmetic.

CRITICAL THINKING: PRIORITIZING

**D** Present your plan to the class. Explain how you prioritized your water usage.

PRESENTING

# FINAL TASK   Role-Playing a Meeting

> You are going to role-play a government meeting about how to manage the local water supply. In the meeting, you will try to decide how much water each of the different organizations should be allowed to use.

**A** Work in a group of four. Read the situation below and the roles. Assign a role to each member of your group.

> **Situation:** The government built a new dam near a large city, and now the reservoir behind the dam is filling with water. Scientists determined how much water the city can take from the reservoir every year. Now the government will have a meeting to decide how to use that water.

> **Role #1:   Manager of the City Water Company**
>
> • The population of the city has increased by 200,000 people in the last 10 years.
> • Now there are strict rules about using water for gardens and washing cars.
> • The price of water is very high.
>
> Requested share: 30 percent of the total amount

**Role #2:   President of the National Farmers' Association**

- Most farms are very small, and farmers don't earn much money.
- With more water, farmers could start growing cotton to sell to other countries.
- Farmers have had problems because there has been very little rain during the past few years.

Requested share: 60 percent of the total amount

**Role #3:   President of the International Aluminum Company**

- The company wants to build a large aluminum[1] factory next to the reservoir.
- The factory would provide new jobs for more than 1,000 people.
- This would be the biggest factory in the region.

Requested share: 50 percent of the total amount

[1]**aluminum** (n): a lightweight metal with many uses

**Role #4:   Director of the National Parks Service**

- Several kinds of rare fish and birds live in lakes that are connected to the reservoir.
- Foreign tourists often come to see and photograph these animals. The tourist industry is important to the local economy.
- If there isn't enough water, all the animals will die, and tourists will stop coming.

Requested share: 20 percent of the total amount

ORGANIZING IDEAS   **B**   Prepare a one-minute talk to introduce your organization and present your viewpoint to the other members of your group. Take notes to help you remember your ideas. Your talk should answer these questions:

- Who are you? What organization or company do you work for?
- How much water does your organization need?
- Why does it need this amount of water?

**C**   With your group, role-play the meeting. Take turns presenting your organizations and viewpoints. Decide how much water each organization will get. The amount must total 100 percent. Then report your group's decision to the class.

# REFLECTION

1. What are two phrases you learned in this unit to help you express your opinion?

_____

_____

2. What is the most useful thing you learned in this unit?

_____

_____

3. Here are the vocabulary words from the unit. Check (✓) the ones you can use.

| | | |
|---|---|---|
| ☐ adequate AWL | ☐ distribute AWL | ☐ resource AWL |
| ☐ agriculture | ☐ experience | ☐ risk |
| ☐ amount | ☐ extremely | ☐ scarce |
| ☐ average | ☐ flow | ☐ significant AWL |
| ☐ collect | ☐ manage | ☐ supply |
| ☐ conservation | ☐ reduce | ☐ urgent |
| ☐ crisis | ☐ require AWL | |

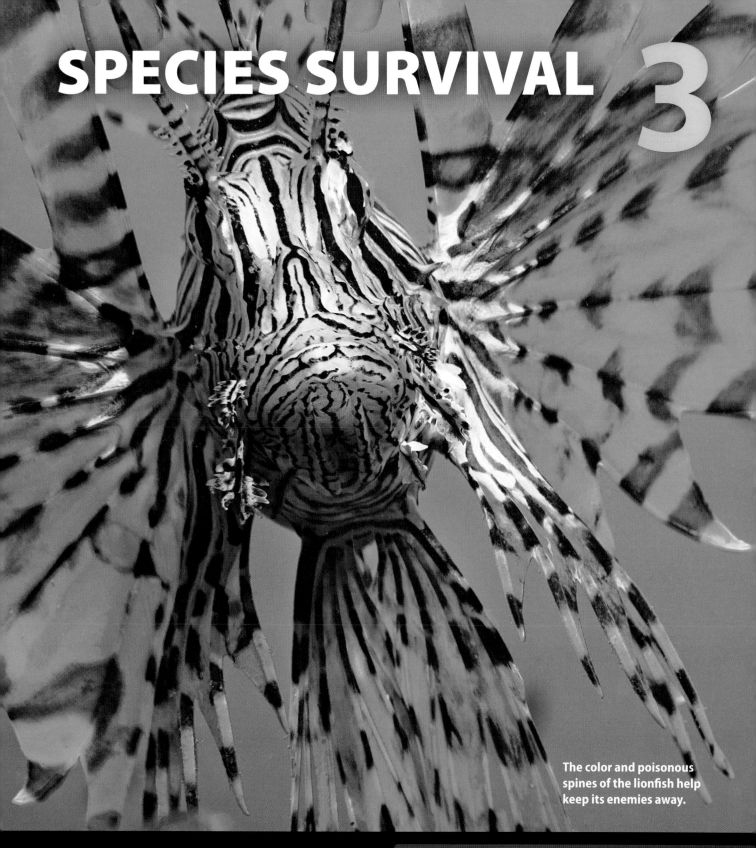

# SPECIES SURVIVAL

# 3

The color and poisonous spines of the lionfish help keep its enemies away.

THINK AND DISCUSS

1  Look at the photo. What helps this fish survive, or live?
2  Look at the title of this unit. What do you think it means?
3  Do you enjoy learning about animals? Why or why not?

**Look at the photos and read the information.
Then discuss these questions.**

1. What are some ways that animals use color in order to survive?

2. What are two ways that the giraffe's long neck helps it survive?

3. Which of the animals on these pages do you find most interesting? Why?

4. Can you think of any other animals that have adapted in some way in order to survive?

# AMAZING ANIMAL ADAPTATIONS

**The lichen katydid from Central and South America uses its perfect camouflage to hide from predators. It looks exactly like the lichen it eats.**

A male Wilson's bird-of-paradise displays his colors to attract a female. Finding a mate will allow him to pass on his genes and help the species continue.

The strawberry poison dart frog's bright colors tell its predators (animals that eat other animals) that it's poisonous and not safe to eat.

The giraffe's long neck is one of the adaptations that helps it survive. Having a very long neck enables it to reach leaves at the tops of trees and see predators from far away.

# A Vocabulary

MEANING FROM CONTEXT **A** 🎧 **Track 14** Look at the map, and read and listen to the information. Notice each word in **blue** and think about its meaning.

## THE *BEAGLE* IN SOUTH AMERICA

The *Beagle* expedition's priority was to map the harbors and coastlines of South America. Charles Darwin also spent a lot of his time on land, exploring parts of the Argentine Pampas, the Atacama Desert, and the Andes mountains.

**1** **Argentina, 1832:** At both Punta Alta and Monte Hermoso, Darwin found fossils of large prehistoric animals. He could not **identify** the fossils, but they were similar to modern animal **species** from the area. This might have been the beginning of his now famous idea that species could change over time.

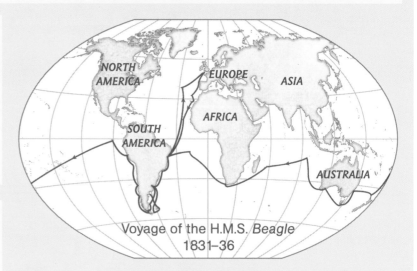

Voyage of the H.M.S. *Beagle* 1831–36

**2** **Chile, 1833:** In South America, the men on Darwin's ship the *Beagle* sometimes ate a bird called a *rhea*. Darwin heard about a smaller type of rhea. It lived mostly in southern Patagonia, while the larger rhea lived in the north. Darwin wondered why the southern rhea **differed** from the northern one. At this time, Darwin became interested in the **diversity** of animal life. Could an animal's environment affect **traits** such as size?

**3** **Galápagos Islands, Ecuador, 1835:** Here, Darwin began to develop his ideas about why and how the diversity of species occurred. In a **process** he called natural selection, an animal with a useful trait was more likely to survive, and therefore, more likely to **reproduce**. The animal's **offspring** would then **inherit** the useful trait. In contrast, animals of that same species with a different trait might die and not reproduce. In this way, a species would **adapt** to its environment and change over time.

**B** Write each word in **blue** from exercise A next to its definition.

1. _____ (v) was unlike something else

2. _____ (v) to recognize someone or something

3. _____ (n) a person's children or an animal's young

4. _____ (n) a variety of things that are different from each other

5. _____ (n) things one gets from one's parents, such as eye color

6. _____ (v) to produce young animals or plants

7. _____ (v) to change in order to be successful in a new situation

8. _____ (n) a certain kind of animal or plant

9. _____ (n) a series of actions or events that leads to a certain result

10. _____ (v) to be born with something because one's parents also had it

**C** 🎧 **Track 15** Read the article and fill in each blank with the correct form of a word from the box. Then listen and check your answers.

| diversity | inherit | process | reproduce | trait |
|---|---|---|---|---|

## OUT OF AFRICA

Anthropologists, scientists who study human beings, have long said that modern humans first lived in Africa and then moved east toward Asia, north across the Mediterranean, and later throughout the world.

Now, a large genetic[1] study supports that theory. The study looked at nearly 1,000 people in 51 places around the world. It found the most genetic

_____ in Africa and
    1

less farther away from Africa. How did this happen? When small groups of people moved away, they took only a small amount of all the possible genetic information with them. People in the small groups

_____. Their offspring _____
  2                3

their parents' more limited set of genes. Therefore,

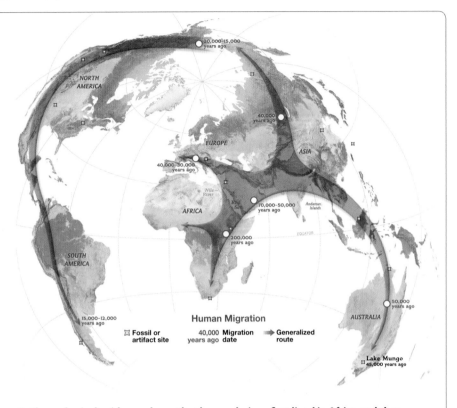

**Human Migration**

⊠ Fossil or artifact site    40,000 years ago Migration date    ➡ Generalized route

**Anthropological evidence shows that human beings first lived in Africa and then moved to different places around the world.**

their _____ were very similar to those of
        4

their parents. This _____ continued as
        5

small groups of people moved farther and farther from Africa.

[1]**genetic** (adj): related to genes (small pieces of DNA) and heredity

**D** Work with a partner. Discuss these questions.

CRITICAL THINKING: ANALYZING

1. How do you differ from other people in your family? In what ways are you similar?
2. What are some of the traits you inherited from your parents and grandparents?
3. What are some species of animals that live in your country?
4. Can you identify many species of birds? Of plants? Explain.
5. What parts of the world have a large diversity of plant and animal species?

# A Listening A Talk about Birds

## BEFORE LISTENING

PRIOR KNOWLEDGE **A** You are going to listen to a biologist in the UK give a presentation before a bird-watching trip. Discuss these questions with a partner.

1. Bird-watching is a hobby that involves viewing birds outdoors in their natural environment. Do you know anyone who enjoys this hobby?
2. What are some good places in your country to see birds and other animals? Do you enjoy going to those places? Explain.

## WHILE LISTENING

> **LISTENING SKILL** Listening for Repeated Words
>
> Speakers often use repetition to emphasize key points. When you are listening to a talk, pay attention to words (including words from the same family, e.g., *differ, different, difference*) and phrases that the speaker repeats. These are usually ideas that the speaker wants listeners to remember.
>
> *The **males** and **females** of this bird species don't **differ** much in their appearance. But the one we saw in the last slide is definitely a **male**. One **difference** is that the **female's** beak is a little shorter, so she can't reach as many kinds of flower seeds as the **male** can.*
>
> Key point: The males and females of this species have different beaks.

LISTENING FOR MAIN IDEAS **B** 🎧 **Track 16** ▶ **3.1** Listen to the talk. Check (✓) the words when you hear them and notice how the speaker repeats them. Then listen again and check (✓) the speaker's main idea.

☐ goldfinch ☐ trait(s) ☐ seeds ☐ beak ☐ greenfinch

_____ Goldfinches fly to warmer parts of Europe during September and October.

_____ Greenfinches have larger, stronger beaks than goldfinches, so they can eat larger seeds.

_____ Different finches have different traits that help them survive and reproduce.

**A European goldfinch with a seed in its beak sits on a thistle plant.**

**Track 16** Listen to the talk again and complete the notes in the chart below.

| | | |
|---|---|---|
| Type of Finch | goldfinch | |
| Where It Lives | | Most of Europe + NW Africa and Turkey |
| Special Traits | | |
| What It Eats | Male: seeds from inside flower<br>Female: other seeds | |
| Other Habits | | Lives diff. places in diff. seasons<br>Summer: parks & forests<br>Winter: gardens and farm fields |

## AFTER LISTENING

**D** Work with a partner. Compare your notes from exercise C.

**NOTE-TAKING SKILL** Re-Writing Your Notes

Since note-taking is usually done quickly—using only key words and phrases, abbreviations, and symbols—it can be helpful to rewrite your notes in sentence form after class. Rewriting your notes will help you remember key ideas. By doing this, you create a set of notes that are easy to read and study from later.

**Original Notes:** *Lives diff. places in diff. seasons*

**Re-Written Notes:** *The greenfinch doesn't leave the UK in the winter, but it does live in different places during different seasons.*

**E** Re-write your notes from exercise C. Use complete sentences. Then work with a partner and compare your notes.

**F** Discuss these questions in a group.

1. Do you enjoy watching TV shows or documentary films about nature? Explain.
2. Have you ever gone on a nature hike? If so, where did you go, and what kind of wildlife did you see? If not, would you like to do this in the future?

# A Speaking

**A** 🎧 **Track 17** Listen to the following words. Then answer the questions below.

| banana | demand | identify | reproduce |
|---|---|---|---|

1. How many syllables are in each word?
2. Which is the stressed syllable in each word?
3. How many different vowel sounds are in each word?

---

**PRONUNCIATION** Stress in Multi-Syllable Words

🎧 **Track 18**

**Primary Stress**

In words with two or more syllables, one syllable is stressed, or stronger than the others. It has a full vowel sound.

| **lo** cal | **fac** tor | **sea** son |
|---|---|---|
| /oʊ/ | /æ/ | /i/ |

**Secondary Stress**

Sometimes in a word with more than two syllables, another syllable is also stressed, but not as fully as the syllable with primary stress. In *analyze*, for example, the primary stress is on the first syllable, and the third syllable has the secondary stress. It has the full vowel sound /aɪ/.

**a** na lyze
/aɪ/

**Unstressed Syllables**

Syllables without stress are said more quickly, and often have the schwa /ə/ sound.

| **lo** cal | **fac** tor | **sea** son |
|---|---|---|
| /ə/ | /ə/ | /ə/ |

---

**B** 🎧 **Track 19** Listen to the words below. Underline the stressed syllable(s) in each word. Then take turns saying the words with a partner.

1. practical
2. compare
3. attachment
4. available
5. proportion
6. support

**C** 🎧 **Track 20** Listen to the words below. Underline the syllable with the most stress in each word. Circle the syllable with secondary stress. Then practice saying the words with a partner.

1. recommend
2. classify
3. atmosphere
4. quantity
5. romantic
6. disappear

CRITICAL THINKING:
ANALYZING

**D** With your partner, analyze your name or the name of a famous person.

1. How many syllables are there?
2. Which syllables have primary or secondary stress?
3. Which syllables are unstressed?
4. Which vowel sounds are full, and which are reduced (schwa) sounds?

We use *because, since,* and *due to (the fact that)* to talk about causes.

> **Since** polar bears live in snowy places, they have developed white fur to help hide them from their prey, or the animals that they kill for food.

We use *so, as a result (of this), therefore,* and *consequently* to talk about effects or results.

> Over time, finches' beaks have become very strong. **As a result,** they can eat hard seeds.

> Polar bears have white fur, **so** their prey doesn't always notice them in the snow and ice.

Polar bears' white fur is a helpful trait because it makes it difficult for their prey (the animals they eat) to see them in the snow.

**E** 🎧 **Track 21** Read and listen to the information about the process of natural selection. Write down the words and phrases you hear that signal causes and effects.

---

**The Process of Natural Selection**

1. First, the environment affects animals in some way.

2. _____ , the animals that have certain helpful traits do well in their environments.

3. And _____ , they survive and reproduce.

4. The offspring of these animals inherit the helpful trait from their parents.

5. This process continues and _____ , over time, most of the animals in the species have the helpful trait.

---

**F** With a partner, explain the process of natural selection using the sentences and the signal words and phrases you wrote in exercise E.

> **>** *Because the environment affects animals in some way, species develop certain helpful traits.*

**G** Work with a partner. Look at the photos and read the information. Then discuss these questions.

1. What are the threats, or dangers, to each animal's survival?
2. What does each animal do in response to these dangers?
3. Which animal behavior is the most surprising or interesting to you? Explain.

## ANIMAL SURVIVAL BEHAVIORS

**Speed:** The blue wildebeest of southern, central, and eastern Africa is a favorite food for lions, leopards, and other large predators. It's also one of the fastest land animals with a top speed of about 50 mph (80 kph)—just a little faster than its predators, most of the time.

**Surprise:** The Texas horned lizard can actually shoot a stream of blood from its eyes when it is disturbed by predators such as snakes, hawks, and coyotes[1]. The surprise can be enough to give the lizard a chance to escape.

**Camouflage:** The dead leaf butterfly lives in tropical parts of Asia. When its wings are open, it's colorful and beautiful. But when its wings are closed, it looks exactly like a dead leaf, which birds and other hungry insects are not interested in eating.

**Playing Dead:** The opossum of North America is nocturnal (active at night) and lives in trees. In addition, if it is disturbed by people, cats, or other predators, it can "play dead"—and even smell bad! It's enough to make anyone walk away!

[1] **coyotes** (n): a kind of North American wild dog

**H** With your partner, take turns finishing these sentences about the animals in exercise G. Then say some sentences using your own ideas.

> *Since lions like to eat blue wildebeests, …the wildebeests need to run very fast.*

1. Since lions and leopards eat blue wildebeests, . . .
2. The butterfly looks like a dead leaf, so . . .
3. The lizard can surprise its predators; as a result, . . .
4. The opossum has several survival behaviors. Consequently, . . .
5. Because the opossum seems to be dead, . . .

**I** With your partner, talk about some other animals you know about (including your own pets if you have any). What survival behaviors do they use? Use words and phrases to talk about causes and effects.

TALKING ABOUT CAUSES AND EFFECTS

> *Because birds can fly, cats and other animals can't catch them.*

## LESSON TASK Presenting a Life Lesson

**A** Work with a partner. Read the information below. Then discuss this question: What are some ways that our human intelligence has helped us survive (e.g., getting food, traveling over long distances)?

CRITICAL THINKING: ANALYZING

> One of the most important human traits is intelligence. Our large brains have allowed us to survive and adapt to our environment in different ways. Some other animals are also quite intelligent, but human beings' ability to create and have an impact on the world sets us apart from other species.

**B** You are going to give a short, informal presentation about a helpful life lesson you have learned. Follow these steps:

ORGANIZING IDEAS

1. Brainstorm some important life lessons you have learned from your family that have helped make your life better in some way. Then choose one of the life lessons from your list.
2. In your notebook, write brief notes about the life lesson you chose. Answer these questions in your notes:

   • What was the lesson?

   • Who did you learn this lesson from?

   • When did you learn this lesson? (How old were you? When did it happen?)

   • Has your life been different as a result of this lesson? How?

**C** Work in a group. Take turns presenting your life lessons. Practice using expressions for talking about causes and effects.

PRESENTING

> *My mother taught me not to form opinions about people too quickly. When I was six, I decided that I didn't like the girl next door even though I didn't know her. I told my mother this, and the next day she invited the girl and her mother over to our house for lunch. We've been best friends ever since…*

Video

# Amazing Chameleons

**Panther chameleon, Madagascar**

## BEFORE VIEWING

MEANING FROM
CONTEXT

**A** Read the information. Notice each underlined word and think about its meaning.

---

### KEYS TO CHAMELEON SURVIVAL

**Skin:** Chameleons' best-known ability is being able to change their skin color. We used to think they did this mostly for camouflage, to match their <u>background</u> and avoid being seen by predators.

**Eyes:** Chameleons' eyes can <u>rotate</u> independently, with one eye looking in one direction and the other eye in another direction.

**Feet:** The shape of chameleons' feet allows them to hold onto tree <u>branches</u>.

**Tongue:** Chameleons have long tongues that they can <u>project</u> out of their mouths at high speeds to catch insects.

**Movements:** Chameleons move in a slow, deliberate way in order to <u>mimic</u> the movement of leaves in the wind—a kind of behavioral camouflage.

---

**B** Write each underlined word from exercise A next to its definition. You may use a dictionary.

1. _____ (n) the smaller parts of trees that grow out from the trunk

2. _____ (v) to turn with a circular movement

3. _____ (v) to imitate or pretend to be something we are not

4. _____ (v) to throw or cause to move forward

5. _____ (n) the surroundings or scene behind something

# WHILE VIEWING

**C** ▶ `3.2` Read the statements. Then watch the video and choose T for *True* or F for *False*. Correct the false statements.

UNDERSTANDING MAIN IDEAS

1. For chameleons, changing colors is a communication strategy.   T   F

2. Female chameleons change colors when they are interested in a male.   T   F

3. Chameleons move in a way that mimics their predators.   T   F

4. Scientists are still learning about chameleons.   T   F

**D** ▶ `3.2` Watch the video again and fill in each blank with the number you hear.

UNDERSTANDING DETAILS

1. Of the _____ chameleon species …, _____ percent occur on Madagascar.

2. Chameleons can project their tongues up to _____ body lengths.

3. This is done at speeds of about _____ miles per hour.

4. _____ percent of chameleon species are threatened with extinction (in danger of dying out or becoming extinct).

5. There are _____ species which are regarded as critically endangered, and _____ species that are regarded as endangered.

# AFTER VIEWING

**E** Work in a group. Read the information. Then discuss the questions below.

CRITICAL THINKING: ANALYZING

> **THREATS TO CHAMELEON SURVIVAL**
>
> **Changes to Habitat:** Human activity results in changes to the places where chameleons live.
>
> **Deforestation:** Trees are cut down and removed by people.
>
> **Range Restriction:** Some chameleons are found only in one specific location. They don't live in many parts of Madagascar.
>
> **Other Pressures on Habitat:** Factors such as climate conditions, farming, and a growing human population can make it more difficult for chameleons to survive.

1. Which of the threats to chameleon survival are directly related to human activity?
2. What are some ways that people could help reduce some of these threats to chameleon survival?
3. Some people keep chameleons as pets. How do you feel about this? Would you want to have a chameleon as a pet? Explain.

# Vocabulary

**A** 🎧 **Track 22** Read and listen to the article. Notice each word in **blue** and think about its meaning.

## BAR CODING LIFE ON EARTH

Paul Hebert is a biologist at the University of Guelph in Canada. As a young man in the 1970s, part of his job was to **classify** thousands of different species of moths[1]. Finding tiny **variations** in the moths in order to describe each species scientifically was not easy, however.

In 2003, Hebert suggested something a bit **controversial**. Instead of using descriptions to identify different species, why not use DNA? Hebert **argued** that a bar code—similar to the bar codes on products in a store—could be created for every living thing on Earth. This was a major break from scientific tradition.

Hebert suggested using part of a **gene** called *CO1*, which nearly every form of life has, to create bar codes. This gene is made up of four chemical **substances** known as *G, T, C,* and *A,* and the **sequence** of these substances differs for each species. Using bar codes and an electronic catalog, scientists or anyone else can identify a plant or animal by testing a **sample** of its DNA.

Hebert's bar code **technique** is not only a good way to identify species, the electronic catalog has also become a public resource that makes people more **aware** of biodiversity[2].

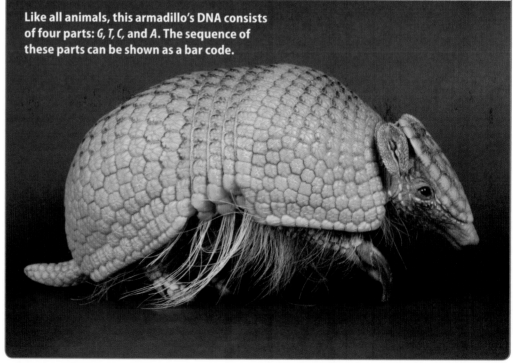

**Like all animals, this armadillo's DNA consists of four parts: *G, T, C,* and *A.* The sequence of these parts can be shown as a bar code.**

[1]**moth** (n): a winged insect that is similar to a butterfly
[2]**biodiversity** (n): many kinds of plants and animals existing in the environment

**B** Complete each sentence with the correct form of a word in **blue** from exercise A.

1. Most people aren't _____ (adj) of the number of species on Earth.

2. Paul Hebert thinks it's difficult to _____ (v) all the species using descriptions.

3. In some cases, there are only very small _____ (n) between one species and another.

4. A different _____ (n) for classifying species is to use their DNA.

5. Hebert's technique is somewhat _____ (adj). Some people don't agree with it.

6. DNA can be taken from a small blood _____ (n).

7. The _____ (n) that researchers are using is called *CO1*.

8. *G, T, C,* and *A* are the _____ (n) that make up DNA.

9. Different _____ (n) of *G, T, C,* and *A* carry different genetic information.

10. Hebert _____ (v) that all species on Earth should be bar coded.

**C** Work with a partner. Take turns asking and answering these questions.

CRITICAL THINKING: ANALYZING

1. What's one technique you use for learning new vocabulary words?
2. Which genes do you think you inherited from your mother or from your father?
3. What's a controversial topic in your country or in the news today?
4. What can be done to make people more aware of endangered species?

---

**VOCABULARY SKILL** Identifying the Correct Definition

Many words in English have more than one meaning. Dictionaries list the most frequently used definition first, but it's important to read all of the possible definitions so you can identify the correct one. Use information provided in the dictionary such as the part of speech and the example sentences to help you.

**sub·stance** /ˈsʌbstəns/ *n.* **1** [U] anything one can touch: *This face cream is a white, sticky substance.*||*Tires are made of rubber and other substances.* **2** *usu. sing.* [C;U] meaning, truth: *What she says has substance because of her knowledge and experience.* **3** [U] wealth, possessions: *The family owns a successful business; they are people of substance.*

THESAURUS **substance 1** material, matter, stuff *infrml.* **2** significance **3** means, resources.

---

**D** Work with a partner. Discuss these questions.

1. Look at the dictionary definition. In the article on page 54, which definition of *sample* does the author use? _____

2. Look up each word in a dictionary. How many definitions do you find for each word?

argue (v) _____     nail (n) _____

fair (adj) _____     draft (n) _____

bear (v) _____

**sam·ple** /ˈsæmpəl/ *v.* [T] **-pled, -pling, -ples** to try *s.t.*: *I sampled each dessert on the menu.*||*I sampled life in Hong Kong and loved it.* —*n.* **1** a single thing that shows what a larger group is like: *The tailor showed us samples of silk, wool, and cotton.* **2** a small amount of *s.t.* to try: *The clerk gave me a sample of cheese to taste; it was so delicious that I bought a pound.* **3** a small part of a larger group, used to study the larger group: *The teacher asked a sample of students if the school should build a new library.*

THESAURUS **sample** *v.* to taste, test. —*n.* **1** an example, a specimen, swatch | piece **2** a taste, trial amount **3** a cross section, subgroup.

# Listening A Conversation about a Photo Project

## BEFORE LISTENING

PRIOR KNOWLEDGE

**A** Read the information about photographer Joel Sartore. Then discuss the questions with a partner.

> **JOEL SARTORE** is a National Geographic photographer. He grew up in Nebraska in the United States His family loved nature and enjoyed spending time outdoors together. He remembers receiving a book about birds as a gift from his mother. In the part of the book about extinction[1], there was a picture of a passenger pigeon called Martha—the last living member of her species. Says Sartore about the disappearance of these birds, "I was amazed that you could go from billions to none."

[1]**extinction** (n): the death of all members of a species

1. What animal species can you name that have gone extinct? What do you know about the causes of their extinction?
2. What are some endangered animal species you know and care about? For example, are you concerned about the survival of polar bears, tigers, or other animals?

## WHILE LISTENING

LISTENING FOR MAIN IDEAS

**B** 🎧 **Track 23** Read each statement. Then listen to the conversation and choose T for *True* or F for *False*. Correct the false statements.

1. Joel Sartore wants to photograph all of the world's animal species.     T     F

2. Sartore wants to photograph the animals before some of them become extinct.     T     F

3. His Photo Ark images show animals in their natural habitats.     T     F

4. The photos Sartore takes are making people more aware of endangered species.     T     F

**A critically endangered red ruffed lemur photographed by Joel Sartore at the Plzen Zoo in the Czech Republic**

National Geographic photographer Joel Sartore photographs a gray wolf on the beach on Vargas Island, British Columbia, Canada.

**C** 🎧 **Track 23** Listen to the conversation again. Which of these points do the speakers make? Choose Y for *Yes* or N for *No* for each statement.

LISTENING FOR DETAILS

1. Sartore is publishing more photos now than he used to.          Y     N
2. Sartore's photographic techniques require natural light.          Y     N
3. Sartore can't possibly photograph every animal species.          Y     N
4. Sartore's photo of a bird helped wildlife groups get more money from the government.          Y     N

## AFTER LISTENING

**CRITICAL THINKING**     Personalizing

When you personalize information, you think about it in relation to yourself, your life, and your knowledge and experiences. Personalizing information helps you to internalize it and process it more deeply. You are also more likely to remember information that is connected to you in some way.

**D** Work in a group. Discuss these questions.

PERSONALIZING

1. Based on your knowledge, do you think the extinction of animal species is a major problem for human beings, or are there other problems we should be more concerned about? Explain.
2. How do you feel when you hear about an endangered species? Are there any species you care more about than others? Explain.
3. Is there anything you are doing now or plan to do in the future to help protect endangered species? For example, are there any products or foods you avoid? Other actions you can take? Explain.

# Speaking

## GRAMMAR FOR SPEAKING Phrasal Verbs

Phrasal verbs are formed with a verb plus a particle, for example, *up, down, in, out,* and *at.*

> Stanley **gets up** at five thirty every morning.
>
> She **looked up** the meaning of the word.

Phrasal verbs have their own meanings. These meanings are different from the usual meaning of the verb plus a preposition.

Phrasal verbs can be transitive or intransitive.

| Transitive | Intransitive |
|---|---|
| Victor **wrote down** the information. | The finches **come back** in the spring. |

Some transitive verbs can be separated from their particles while others cannot.

| Separable | Inseparable |
|---|---|
| Please **turn down** the volume. | √ Jemila really **takes after** her mother. |
| Please **turn** the volume **down**. | X Jemila really ~~takes her mother after~~. |

**A** 🎧 **Track 24** Read and listen to the phone conversation. Notice the underlined phrasal verbs and think about their meanings.

| | |
|---|---|
| **Matt:** | Jessica? It's me! |
| **Jessica:** | Matt! It's great to hear your voice! Are you back home now? |
| **Matt:** | Yes, and I really missed you, but I'm so happy you <u>talked</u> me <u>into</u> going on the expedition! I can't believe I almost <u>turned down</u> such a great opportunity. |
| **Jessica:** | Tell me all about it! |
| **Matt:** | Well, we were high up in the Foja Mountains. No human beings have ever lived there! |
| **Jessica:** | How exciting! Did you get a lot of work done? |
| **Matt:** | We did! We <u>set up</u> a tent as our laboratory. It was small but fine. |
| **Jessica:** | Did it rain a lot? |
| **Matt:** | Every day. Well—one afternoon the sky <u>cleared up</u> for a while, but the clouds were back by that evening. It was OK, though. The frogs didn't mind the rain. |
| **Jessica:** | Oh, tell me about the frogs! |
| **Matt:** | Can you believe there are 350 frog species in New Guinea? The best time to find them is at night. When I <u>turned on</u> my flashlight, I could see them easily and <u>pick</u> them <u>up</u> with my hands. |
| **Jessica:** | How interesting! It sounds like it was a great trip. |
| **Matt:** | It was, and the lead scientist was really happy with my work. |
| **Jessica:** | That's great! Congratulations, Matt! |

A spurred big-eyed tree frog from New Guinea's Foja Mountains

**B** Work with a partner. Discuss the meanings of the phrasal verbs from exercise A.

**C** Practice the conversation from exercise A with your partner. Then switch roles and practice it again.

**D** Complete each statement with the correct form of a phrasal verb from exercise A.

1. I didn't want to do it, but my friend _____ me _____ it.

2. Your bag is on the floor. You should _____ it _____. The floor in here is very dirty!

3. Let's _____ the laboratory for our experiment so that it's ready tomorrow.

4. It was raining this morning, but now the sky has _____.

5. When I drive to work, I always _____ the radio and listen to the news.

6. I _____ Lara's invitation to go to the movies tonight because I have to study for the test tomorrow.

> **EVERYDAY LANGUAGE**   Congratulating Someone
>
> *Well done!*        *Congratulations!*        *I'm happy for you!*        *Way to go!*

## FINAL TASK  Presenting a Research Proposal

> You are going to collaborate in a group to plan a research proposal. You will then present your proposal as a group to the class.

**A** Work in a group. Read the information and follow the steps on the next page.

> **Situation:** Your group is going on a scientific research field trip! And the best news is that you have received a government research grant, so you have plenty of travel money. However, before you actually receive the grant money, you must submit your research proposal.

1. Brainstorm a list of several interesting places you might go to do your research. What could you research in those places (e.g., what species of plants or animals)? Choose one of the ideas from your list, and write it in your Research Proposal.

Research Proposal

A. Destination: _____

B. Research Topic: _____

2. Think about and discuss what you will need in order to travel to your destination and do your research.

C. Travel Plans: _____

D. Equipment Requests: _____

3. Because you're getting a government grant, you'll be expected to do something with your research after you return home. How will you use your research?

E. Follow-Up Plans: _____

**PRESENTATION SKILL** Timing Your Presentation

Presentations often have a time requirement or a time limit. When you plan and practice your presentation, it's important to know how long your presentation needs to be. You want to be sure your presentation is long enough but doesn't go over the time limit. When you're planning a group presentation, first decide how much time each person needs for their part of the presentation. Practice and time yourself speaking individually, and then practice your presentation as a group.

ORGANIZING IDEAS **B** Find out how much time you will have to present your research proposal. Decide which information each member of your group will present. Each person should plan to include some details about the information that he or she will present. Then practice and time your presentation.

PRESENTING **C** Present your research plan to the class.

# REFLECTION

1. When are you likely to use the expressions for talking about causes and effects?

_____

_____

2. How did the information about species survival in this unit change or add to your ideas about wildlife?

_____

_____

3. Here are the vocabulary words from the unit. Check (✓) the ones you can use.

| | | |
|---|---|---|
| ☐ adapt AWL | ☐ gene | ☐ sequence AWL |
| ☐ argue | ☐ identify AWL | ☐ species |
| ☐ aware AWL | ☐ inherit | ☐ substance |
| ☐ classify | ☐ offspring | ☐ technique AWL |
| ☐ controversial AWL | ☐ process AWL | ☐ trait |
| ☐ differ | ☐ reproduce | ☐ variation AWL |
| ☐ diversity AWL | ☐ sample | |

# Independent Student Handbook

**Table of Contents**

## LISTENING SKILLS

### Predicting

Speakers giving formal talks usually begin by introducing themselves and their topic. Listen carefully to the introduction of the topic so that you can predict what the talk will be about.

**Strategies:**

- Use visual information including titles on the board or on presentation slides.
- Think about what you already know about the topic.
- Ask yourself questions that you think the speaker might answer.
- Listen for specific phrases that indicate an introduction (e.g., *My topic is…*).

### Listening for Main Ideas

It's important to be able to tell the difference between a speaker's main ideas and supporting details. It is more common for teachers to test students' understanding of main ideas than of specific details.

**Strategies:**

- Listen carefully to the introduction. Speakers often state the main idea in the introduction.
- Listen for rhetorical questions, or questions that the speaker asks, and then answers. Often the answer is the statement of the main idea.
- Notice words and phrases that the speaker repeats. Repetition often signals main ideas.

### Listening for Details (Examples)

A speaker often provides examples that support a main idea. A good example can help you understand and remember the main idea better.

**Strategies:**

- Listen for specific phrases that introduce examples.
- Listen for general statements. Examples often follow general statements.

### Listening for Details (Reasons)

Speakers often give reasons or list causes and/or effects to support their ideas.

**Strategies:**

- Notice nouns that might signal causes/reasons (e.g., *factors, influences, causes, reasons*) or effects/results (e.g., *effects, results, outcomes, consequences*).
- Notice verbs that might signal causes/reasons (e.g., *contribute to, affect, influence, determine, produce, result in*) or effects/results (often these are passive, e.g., *is affected by*).

## Understanding the Structure of a Presentation

An organized speaker uses expressions to alert the audience to important information that will follow. Recognizing signal words and phrases will help you understand how a presentation is organized and the relationship between ideas.

### Introduction

A good introduction identifies the topic and gives an idea of how the lecture or presentation will be organized. Here are some expressions to introduce a topic:

*I'll be talking about . . .*  *My topic is . . .*

*There are basically two groups . . .*  *There are three reasons . . .*

### Body

In the body of a lecture, speakers usually expand upon the topic. They often use phrases that signal the order of events or subtopics and their relationship to each other. Here are some expressions to help listeners follow the body of a lecture:

*The first/next/final (point/reason) is . . .*  *First/Next/Finally, let's look at . . .*

*Another reason is . . .*  *However, . . .*

### Conclusion

In the conclusion of a lecture, speakers often summarize what they have said. They may also make predictions or suggestions. Sometimes they ask a question in the conclusion to get the audience to think more about the topic. Here are some expressions to give a conclusion:

*In conclusion, . . .*  *In summary, . . .*

*As you can see. . .*  *To review, + (restatement of main points)*

## Understanding Meaning from Context

When you are not familiar with a word that a speaker says, you can sometimes guess the meaning of the word or fill in the gaps using the context or situation itself.

**Strategies:**

- Don't panic. You don't always understand every word of what a speaker says in your first language, either.
- Use context clues to fill in the blanks. What did you understand just before or just after the missing part? What did the speaker probably say?
- Listen for words and phrases that signal a definition or explanation (e.g., *What that means is…*).

## Recognizing a Speaker's Bias

Speakers often have an opinion about the topic they are discussing. It's important for you to know if they are objective or subjective about the topic. Objective speakers do not express an opinion. Subjective speakers have a bias or a strong feeling about the topic.

### Strategies:

- Notice words like adjectives, adverbs, and modals that the speaker uses (e.g., *ideal, horribly, should, shouldn't*). These suggest that the speaker has a bias.
- Listen to the speaker's voice. Does he or she sound excited, angry, or bored?
- Notice if the speaker gives more weight or attention to one point of view over another.
- Listen for words that signal opinions (e.g., *I think…*).

# NOTE-TAKING SKILLS

Taking notes is a personalized skill. It is important to develop a note-taking system that works for you. However, there are some common strategies to improve your note taking.

## Before You Listen

### Focus

Try to clear your mind before the speaker begins so you can pay attention. If possible, review previous notes or think about what you already know about the topic.

### Predict

If you know the topic of the talk, think about what you might hear.

## Listen

### Take Notes by Hand

Research suggests that taking notes by hand rather than on a computer is more effective. Taking notes by hand requires you to summarize, rephrase, and synthesize information. This helps you *encode* the information, or put it into a form that you can understand and remember.

### Listen for Signal Words and Phrases

Speakers often use signal words and phrases (e.g., *Today we're going to talk about…*) to organize their ideas and show relationships between them. Listening for signal words and phrases can help you decide what information to write in your notes.

### Condense (Shorten) Information

- As you listen, focus on the most important ideas. The speaker will usually repeat, define, explain, and/or give examples of these ideas. Take notes on these ideas.

    Speaker: *The Itaipu Dam provides about 20% of the electricity used in Brazil, and about 75% of the electricity used in Paraguay. That electricity goes to millions of homes and businesses, so it's good for the economy of both countries.*

    Notes: Itaipu Dam → electricity: Brazil 20%, Paraguay 75%

- Don't write full sentences. Write only key words (nouns, verbs, adjectives, and adverbs), phrases, or short sentences.

    Full sentence: *Teachers are normally at the top of the list of happiest jobs.*

    Notes: teachers happiest

- Leave out information that is obvious.

    Full sentence: *Photographer Annie Griffiths is famous for her beautiful photographs. She travels all over the world to take photos.*

    Notes: A. *Griffiths travels world*

- Write numbers and statistics. (*9 bil; 35%*)
- Use abbreviations (e.g., *ft., min., yr*) and symbols (=, ≠, >, <, %, →)
- Use indenting. Write main ideas on the left side of the paper. Indent details.
    *Benefits of eating ugly foods*
        *Save $*
            *10-20% on ugly fruits & vegs. at market*
- Write details under key terms to help you remember them.
- Write the definitions of important new words.

## After You Listen

- Review your notes soon after the lecture or presentation. Add any details you missed.
- Clarify anything you don't understand in your notes with a classmate or teacher.
- Add or highlight main ideas. Cross out details that aren't important or necessary.
- Rewrite anything that is hard to read or understand. Rewrite your notes in an outline or other graphic organizer to organize the information more clearly.
- Use arrows, boxes, diagrams, or other visual cues to show relationships between ideas.

# ORGANIZING INFORMATION

You can use a graphic organizer to take notes while you are listening, or to organize your notes after you listen. Here are some examples of graphic organizers:

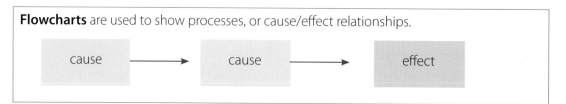

**Flowcharts** are used to show processes, or cause/effect relationships.

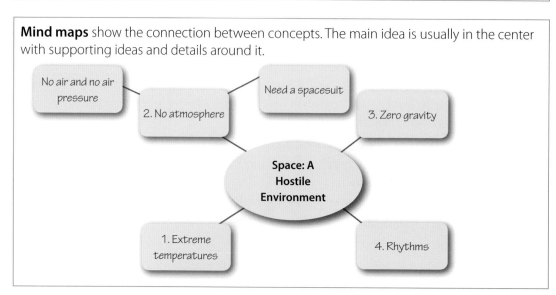

**Mind maps** show the connection between concepts. The main idea is usually in the center with supporting ideas and details around it.

**Outlines** show the relationship between main ideas and details.

To use an outline for taking notes, write the main ideas at the left margin of your paper. Below the main ideas, indent and write the supporting ideas and details. You may do this as you listen, or go back and rewrite your notes as an outline later.

I. **Introduction:** How to feed the world

II. **Steps**

Step One: Stop deforestation

a. stop burning rainforests

b. grow crops on land size of South America

**T-charts** compare two topics.

| Climate Change in Greenland | |
|---|---|
| **Benefits** | **Drawbacks** |
| shorter winters | rising sea levels |

**Timelines** show a sequence of events.

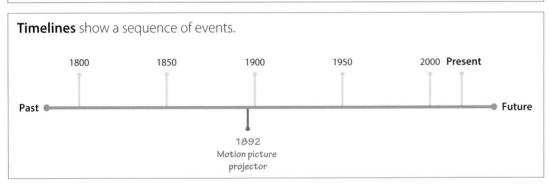

**Venn diagrams** compare and contrast two or more topics. The overlapping areas show similarities.

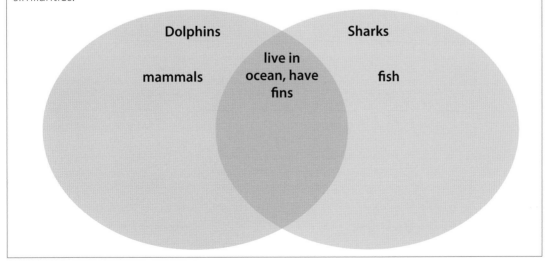

# SPEAKING: PHRASES FOR CLASSROOM COMMUNICATION

| Phrases for Expressing Yourself | |
|---|---|
| **Expressing Opinions**<br>*I think…*<br>*I believe…*<br>*I'm sure…*<br>*In my opinion/view…*<br>*If you ask me,…*<br>*Personally,…*<br>*To me,…* | **Expressing Likes and Dislikes**<br>*I like…*<br>*I prefer…*<br>*I love…*<br>*I can't stand…*<br>*I hate…*<br>*I really don't like…*<br>*I don't care for…* |
| **Giving Facts**<br>*There is evidence/proof…*<br>*Experts claim/argue…*<br>*Studies show…*<br>*Researchers found…*<br>*The record shows…* | **Giving Tips or Suggestions**<br>*Imperatives (e.g., Try to get more sleep.)*<br>*You/We should/shouldn't…*<br>*You/We ought to…*<br>*It's (not) a good idea to…*<br>*I suggest (that)…*<br>*Let's…*<br>*How about… + (noun/gerund)*<br>*What about… + (noun/gerund)*<br>*Why don't we/you…*<br>*You/We could…* |
| **Agreeing**<br>*I agree.*<br>*True.*<br>*Good point.*<br>*Exactly.*<br>*Absolutely.*<br>*I was just about to say that.*<br>*Definitely.*<br>*Right!* | **Disagreeing**<br>*I disagree.*<br>*I'm not so sure about that.*<br>*I don't know.*<br>*That's a good point, but I don't agree.*<br>*I see what you mean, but I think that…* |

## Phrases for Interacting with Others

### Clarifying/Checking Your Understanding

*So are you saying that…?*
*So what you mean is…?*
*What do you mean?*
*How's that?*
*How so?*
*I'm not sure I understand/follow.*
*Do you mean…?*
*I'm not sure what you mean.*

### Asking for Clarification/Confirming Understanding

*Sorry, I didn't catch that. Could you repeat it?*
*I'm not sure I understand the question.*
*I'm not sure I understand what you mean.*
*Sorry, I'm not following you.*
*Are you saying that…?*
*If I understand correctly, you're saying that…*
*Oh, now I get it. You're talking about…, right?*

### Checking Others' Understanding

*Does that make sense?*
*Do you understand?*
*Do you see what I mean?*
*Is that clear?*
*Are you following/with me?*
*Do you have any questions?*

### Asking for Opinions

*What do you think?*
*We haven't heard from you in a while.*
*Do you have anything to add?*
*What are your thoughts?*
*How do you feel?*
*What's your opinion?*

### Taking Turns

*Can/May I say something?*
*Could I add something?*
*Can I just say…?*
*May I continue?*
*Can I finish what I was saying?*
*Did you finish your thought?*
*Let me finish.*
*Let's get back to…*

### Interrupting Politely

*Excuse me.*
*Pardon me.*
*Forgive me for interrupting…*
*I hate to interrupt but…*
*Can I stop you for a second?*

### Asking for Repetition

*Could you say that again?*
*I'm sorry?*
*I didn't catch what you said.*
*I'm sorry. I missed that. What did you say?*
*Could you repeat that please?*

### Showing Interest

| | |
|---|---|
| *I see.* | *Good for you.* |
| *Really?* | *Seriously?* |
| *Um-hmm.* | *No kidding!* |
| *Wow.* | *And? (Then what?)* |

*That's funny / amazing / incredible / awful!*

# SPEAKING: PHRASES FOR PRESENTING

## Introduction

### Introducing a Topic

*I'm going to talk about…*

*My topic is…*

*I'm going to present…*

*I plan to discuss…*

*Let's start with…*

*Today we're going to talk about…*

*So we're going to show you…*

*Now/Right/So/Well, (pause), let's look at…*

*There are three groups/reasons/effects/factors…*

*There are four steps in this process.*

## Body

### Listing or Sequencing

*First/First of all/The first (noun)/To start/To begin,…*

*Second/Secondly/The second/Next/Another/Also/Then/In addition,…*

*Last/The last/Finally,…*

*There are many/several/three types/kinds of/ways,…*

### Signaling Problems/Solutions

*One problem/issue/challenge is…*

*One solution/answer/response is…*

### Giving Reasons or Causes

*Because + (clause): Because the climate is changing…*

*Because of + (noun phrase): Because of climate change…*

*Due to + (noun phrase)…*

*Since + (clause)*

*The reason that I like hip-hop is…*

*One reason that people listen to music is…*

*One factor is + (noun phrase)*

*The main reason that…*

### Giving Results or Effects

*so + (clause): so I went to the symphony*

*Therefore, + (sentence): Therefore, I went to the symphony.*

*As a result, + (sentence).*

*Consequently, + (sentence).*

*…causes + (noun phrase)*

*…leads to + (noun phrase)*

*…had an impact/effect on + (noun phrase)*

*If…then…*

### Giving Examples

*The first example is…*

*Here's an example of what I mean…*

*For instance,…*

*For example,…*

*Let me give you an example…*

*…such as…*

*…like…*

### Repeating and Rephrasing

*What you need to know is…*

*I'll say this again…*

*So again, let me repeat…*

*The most important point is…*

| Signaling Additional Examples or Ideas | Signaling to Stop Taking Notes |
|---|---|
| *Not only…but,* | *You don't need this for the test.* |
| *Besides…* | *This information is in your books/on your handout/on the website.* |
| *Not only do…, but also* | *You don't have to write all this down.* |
| **Identifying a Side Track** | **Returning to a Previous Topic** |
| *This is off-topic,…* | *Getting back to our previous discussion,…* |
| *On a different subject,…* | *To return to our earlier topic…* |
| *As an aside, …* | *OK, getting back on topic…* |
| *That reminds me…* | *So to return to what we were saying,…* |
| **Signaling a Definition** | **Talking about Visuals** |
| *Which means…* | *This graph/infographic/diagram shows/explains…* |
| *What that means is…* | *The line/box/image represents…* |
| *Or…* | *The main point of this visual is…* |
| *In other words,…* | *You can see…* |
| *Another way to say that is…* | *From this we can see…* |
| *That is…* | |
| *That is to say…* | |

## Conclusion

| Concluding | |
|---|---|
| *Well/So, that's how I see it.* | *To sum up,* |
| *In conclusion,* | *As you can see,…* |
| *In summary,* | *At the end,…* |
| | *To review, (+ restatement of main points)* |

# PRESENTATION STRATEGIES

You will often have to give individual or group presentations in your class. The strategies below will help you to prepare, present, and reflect on your presentations.

## Prepare

As you prepare your presentation:

### Consider Your Topic

- **Choose a topic you feel passionate about.** If you are passionate about your topic, your audience will be more interested and excited about your topic, too. Focus on one major idea that you can bring to life. The best ideas are the ones your audience wants to experience.

## Consider Your Purpose

- **Have a strong start.** Use an effective hook, such as a quote, an interesting example, a rhetorical question, or a powerful image to get your audience's attention. Include one sentence that explains what you will do in your presentation and why.
- **Stay focused.** Make sure your details and examples support your main points. Avoid sidetracks or unnecessary information that takes you away from your topic.
- **Use visuals that relate to your ideas.** Drawings, photos, video clips, infographics, charts, maps, slides, and physical objects can get your audience's attention and explain ideas effectively. For example, a photo or map of a location you mention can help your audience picture a place they have never been. Slides with only key words and phrases can help emphasize your main points. Visuals should be bright, clear, and simple.
- **Have a strong conclusion.** A strong conclusion should serve the same purpose as a strong start—to get your audience's attention and make them think. Good conclusions often refer back to the introduction, or beginning of the presentation. For example, if you ask a question in the beginning, you can answer it in the conclusion. Remember to restate your main points, and add a conclusion device such as a question, a call to action, or a quote.

## Consider your Audience

- **Use familiar concepts.** Think about the people in your audience. Ask yourself these questions: Where are they from? How old are they? What is their background? What do they already know about my topic? What information do I need to explain? Use language and concepts they will understand.
- **Share a personal story.** Consider presenting information that will get an emotional reaction; for example, information that will make your audience feel surprised, curious, worried, or upset. This will help your audience relate to you and your topic.
- **Be authentic (be yourself!).** Write your presentation yourself. Use words that you know and are comfortable using.

## Rehearse

- **Make an outline** to help you organize your ideas.
- **Write notes on notecards.** Do not write full sentences, just key words and phrases to help you remember important ideas. Mark the words you should stress and places to pause.
- **Review pronunciation.** Check the pronunciation of words you are uncertain about with a classmate, a teacher, or in a dictionary. Note and practice the pronunciation of difficult words.
- **Memorize the introduction and conclusion.** Rehearse your presentation several times. Practice saying it out loud to yourself (perhaps in front of a mirror or video recorder) and in front of others.
- **Ask for feedback.** Note and revise information that doesn't flow smoothly based on feedback and on your own performance in rehearsal. If specific words or phrases are still a problem, rephrase them.

## Present

As you present:

- **Pay attention to your pacing** (how fast or slow you speak). Remember to speak slowly and clearly. Pause to allow your audience to process information.
- **Speak at a volume loud enough to be heard** by everyone in the audience, but not too loud. Ask the audience if your volume is OK at the beginning of your talk.

- **Vary your intonation.** Don't speak in the same tone throughout the talk. Your audience will be more interested if your voice rises and falls, speeds up and slows down to match the ideas you are talking about.
- **Be friendly and relaxed with your audience**—remember to smile!
- **Show enthusiasm for your topic.** Use humor if appropriate.
- **Have a relaxed body posture.** Don't stand with your arms folded, or look down at your notes. Use gestures when helpful to emphasize your points.
- **Don't read directly from your notes.** Use them to help you remember ideas.
- **Don't look at or read from your visuals too much.** Use them to support your ideas.
- **Make frequent eye contact** with the entire audience.

## Reflect

As you reflect on your presentation:

- **Consider what you think went well** during your presentation and what areas you can improve upon.
- **Get feedback** from your classmates and teacher. How do their comments relate to your own thoughts about your presentation? Did they notice things you didn't? How can you use their feedback in your next presentation?

## PRESENTATION OUTLINE

When you are planning a presentation, you may find it helpful to use an outline. If it is a group presentation, the outline can provide an easy way to divide the content. For example, one student can do the introduction, another student the first idea in the body, and so on.

### 1. Introduction

Topic: _____

Hook: _____

Statement of main idea: _____

### 2. Body

First step/example/reason: _____

Supporting details: _____ _____ _____

Second step/example/reason: _____

Supporting details: _____ _____ _____

Third step/example/reason: _____

Supporting details: _____ _____ _____

### 3. Conclusion

Main points to summarize: _____ _____

Suggestions/Predictions: _____ _____

Closing comments/summary: _____ _____

# PRONUNCIATION GUIDE

## Sounds and Symbols

### Vowels

| Symbol | Key Words |
|--------|-----------|
| /ɑ/ | hot, stop |
| /æ/ | cat, ran |
| /aɪ/ | fine, nice |
| /i/ | eat, need |
| /ɪ/ | sit, him |
| /eɪ/ | name, say |
| /ɛ/ | get, bed |
| /ʌ/ | cup, what |
| /ə/ | about, lesson |
| /u/ | boot, new |
| /ʊ/ | book, could |
| /oʊ/ | go, road |
| /ɔ/ | law, walk |
| /aʊ/ | house, now |
| /ɔɪ/ | toy, coin |

### Consonants

| Symbol | Key Word | Symbol | Key Word |
|--------|----------|--------|----------|
| /b/ | boy | /t/ | tea |
| /d/ | day | /tʃ/ | cheap |
| /dʒ/ | job, bridge | /v/ | vote |
| /f/ | face | /w/ | we |
| /g/ | go | /y/ | yes |
| /h/ | hat | /z/ | zoo |
| /k/ | key, car | | |
| /l/ | love | /ð/ | they |
| /m/ | my | /θ/ | think |
| /n/ | nine | /ʃ/ | shoe |
| /ŋ/ | sing | /ʒ/ | measure |
| /p/ | pen | | |
| /r/ | right | | |
| /s/ | see | | |

Source: *The Newbury House Dictionary plus Grammar Reference*, Fifth Edition, National Geographic Learning/Cengage Learning, 2014.

## Rhythm

The rhythm of English involves stress and pausing.

**Stress**

• English words are based on syllables—units of sound that include one vowel sound.

• In every word in English, one syllable has the primary stress.

• In English, speakers group words that go together based on the meaning and context of the sentence. These groups of words are called *thought groups*. In each thought group, one word is stressed more than the others—the stress is placed on the syllable with the primary stress in this word.

• In general, new ideas and information are stressed.

**Pausing**

• Pauses in English can be divided into two groups: long and short pauses.

• English speakers use long pauses to mark the conclusion of a thought, items in a list, or choices given.

• Short pauses are used in between thought groups to break up the ideas in sentences into smaller, more manageable chunks of information.

English speakers use intonation, or pitch (the rise and fall of their voice), to help express meaning. For example, speakers usually use a rising intonation at the end of *yes/no* questions, and a falling intonation at the end of *wh-* questions and statements.

# VOCABULARY BUILDING STRATEGIES

Vocabulary learning is an on-going process. The strategies below will help you learn and remember new vocabulary words.

## Guessing Meaning from Context

You can often guess the meaning of an unfamiliar word by looking at or listening to the words and sentences around it. Speakers usually know when a word is unfamiliar to the audience, or is essential to understanding the main ideas, and often provide clues to its meaning.

- Repetition: A speaker may use the same key word or phrase, or use another form of the same word.
- Restatement or synonym: A speaker may give a synonym to explain the meaning of a word, using phrases such as, *in other words, also called, or…, also known as.*
- Antonyms: A speaker may define a word by explaining what it is NOT. The speaker may say *Unlike A/In contrast to A, B is…*
- Definition: Listen for signals such as *which means* or *is defined as.* Definitions can also be signaled by a pause.
- Examples: A speaker may provide examples that can help you figure out what something is. For example, ***Mascots*** *are a very popular marketing tool. You've seen them on commercials and in ads on social media –* ***cute, brightly colored creatures that help sell a product.***

## Understanding Word Families: Stems, Prefixes, and Suffixes

Use your understanding of stems, prefixes, and suffixes to recognize unfamiliar words and to expand your vocabulary. The stem is the root part of the word, which provides the main meaning. A prefix comes before the stem and usually modifies meaning (e.g., adding *re-* to a word means "again" or "back"). A suffix comes after the stem and usually changes the part of speech (e.g., adding *-ion, -tion,* or *-ation* to a verb changes it to a noun). Words that share the same stem or root belong to the same word family (e.g., *event, eventful, uneventful, uneventfully*).

| Word Stem | Meaning | Example |
| --- | --- | --- |
| *ann, enn* | year | anniversary, millennium |
| *chron(o)* | time | chronological, synchronize |
| *flex, flect* | bend | flexible, reflection |
| *graph* | draw, write | graphics, paragraph |
| *lab* | work | labor, collaborate |
| *mob, mot, mov* | move | automobile, motivate, mover |
| *port* | carry | transport, import |
| *sect* | cut | sector, bisect |

| Prefix | Meaning | Example |
| --- | --- | --- |
| *dis-* | not, opposite of | disappear, disadvantages |
| *in-, im-, il-, ir-* | not | inconsistent, immature, illegal, irresponsible |
| *inter-* | between | Internet, international |
| *mis-* | bad, badly, incorrectly | misunderstand, misjudge |
| *pre-* | before | prehistoric, preheat |
| *re-* | again; back | repeat; return |
| *trans-* | across, beyond | transfer, translate |
| *un-* | not | uncooked, unfair |

| Suffix | Meaning | Example |
| --- | --- | --- |
| *-able, -ible* | worth, ability | believable, impossible |
| *-en* | to cause to become; made of | lengthen, strengthen; golden |
| *-er, -or* | one who | teacher, director |
| *-ful* | full of | beautiful, successful |
| *-ify, -fy* | to make or become | simplify, satisfy |
| *-ion, -tion, -ation* | condition, action | occasion, education, foundation |
| *-ize* | cause | modernize, summarize |
| *-ly* | in the manner of | carefully, happily |
| *-ment* | condition or result | assignment, statement |
| *-ness* | state of being | happiness, sadness |

## Using a Dictionary

Here are some tips for using a dictionary:

- When you see or hear a new word, try to guess its part of speech (noun, verb, adjective, etc.) and meaning, then look it up in a dictionary.
- Some words have multiple meanings. Look up a new word in the dictionary and try choose the correct meaning for the context. Then see if it makes sense within the context.
- When you look up a word, look at all the definitions to see if there is a basic core meaning. This will help you understand the word when it is used in a different context. Also look at all the related words, or words in the same family. This can help you expand your vocabulary. For example, the core meaning of *structure* involves something built or put together.

> **structure** /ˈstrʌktʃər/ *n.* **1** [C] a building of any kind: *A new structure is being built on the corner.* **2** [C] any architectural object of any kind: *The Eiffel Tower is a famous Parisian structure.* **3** [U] the way parts are put together or organized: *the structure of a song‖a business's structure*
> *–v.* [T] **-tured, -turing, -tures** to put together or organize parts of s.t.: *We are structuring a plan to hire new teachers.*
> *-adj.* **structural.**

Source: *The Newbury House Dictionary plus Grammar Reference*, Fifth Edition, National Geographic Learning/Cengage Learning, 2014

## Multi-Word Units

You can improve your fluency if you learn and use vocabulary as multi-word units: idioms (*go the extra mile*), collocations (*wide range*), and fixed expressions (*in other words*). Some multi-word units can only be understood as a chunk – the individual words do not add up to the same overall meaning. Keep track of multi-word units in a notebook or on notecards.

## Vocabulary Note Cards

You can expand your vocabulary by using vocabulary note cards or a vocabulary building app. Write the word, expression, or sentence that you want to learn on one side. On the other, draw a four-square grid and write the following information in the squares: definition; translation (in your first language); sample sentence; synonyms. Choose words that are high frequency or on the academic word list. If you have looked a word up a few times, you should make a card for it.

| definition: | first language translation: |
|---|---|
| sample sentence: | synonyms: |

Organize the cards in review sets so you can practice them. Don't put words that are similar in spelling or meaning in the same review set as you may get them mixed up. Go through the cards and test yourself on the words or expressions. You can also practice with a partner.

# VOCABULARY INDEX

| Word | Page | CEFR† Level | Word | Page | CEFR† Level |
|------|------|-------------|------|------|-------------|
| adapt | 44 | B2 | identify | 44 | B2 |
| adequate* | 24 | B2 | impact* | 14 | B2 |
| agriculture | 34 | B2 | individual | 14 | B1 |
| alternative* | 14 | B2 | inherit | 44 | C2 |
| amount | 24 | B1 | innovative* | 14 | C1 |
| argue | 54 | B1 | instruct* | 4 | C1 |
| artificial | 4 | B2 | intend | 4 | B1 |
| average | 34 | B1 | manage | 24 | B1 |
| aware | 54 | B2 | offspring | 44 | C2 |
| beyond | 4 | B2 | practical | 4 | B2 |
| capable* | 4 | B2 | process | 44 | B2 |
| carbon | 14 | B2 | reduce | 34 | B1 |
| circumstances* | 4 | B2 | reliable | 4 | B1 |
| classify | 54 | C1 | replace* | 4 | B1 |
| collect | 24 | A2 | reproduce | 44 | C1 |
| command | 4 | B2 | require* | 24 | B2 |
| conservation | 34 | B2 | resource* | 24 | B2 |
| consume* | 14 | B2 | risk | 24 | B2 |
| controversial | 54 | B2 | sample | 54 | B2 |
| crisis | 34 | B2 | scarce | 34 | C1 |
| cut back on | 14 | C2 | sequence | 54 | C1 |
| differ | 44 | B2 | significant* | 24 | B2 |
| distribute* | 34 | B2 | species | 44 | B2 |
| diversity | 44 | C1 | substance | 54 | B2 |
| experience* | 34 | B1 | supply | 24 | B2 |
| extremely | 34 | B1 | technique | 54 | B1 |
| flow | 24 | B1 | trait | 44 | C2 |
| fossil fuel | 14 | B1 | urgent | 34 | B1 |
| gene | 54 | C1 | variation | 54 | B2 |
| gradual | 14 | B2 | worldwide | 14 | B2 |

†The Common European Framework of Reference for Languages (CEFR) is an international standard for describing language proficiency.

*These words are on the Academic Word List (AWL). The AWL is a list of the 570 highest-frequency academic word families that regularly appear in academic texts. The AWL was compiled by researcher Averil Coxhead based on her analysis of a 3.5-million-word corpus (Coxhead, 2000).

# NOTES

# NOTES

# NOTES

# NOTES

# NOTES

# NOTES